Our Story

Our Story

A Guide to Recording

and Sharing Your Family History

Rachel F. Seidman

SIMON ELEMENT

New York   Amsterdam/Antwerp   London
Toronto   Sydney/Melbourne   New Delhi

SIMON
ELEMENT

An Imprint of Simon & Schuster, LLC
1230 Avenue of the Americas
New York, NY 10020

Copyright © 2026 by Rachel F. Seidman

First Simon Element hardcover edition May 2026

SIMON ELEMENT and colophon are registered trademarks of Simon & Schuster, LLC

Simon & Schuster strongly believes in freedom of expression and stands against censorship in all its forms. For more information, visit BooksBelong.com.

For information about special discounts for bulk purchases, please contact Simon & Schuster Special Sales at 1-866-506-1949 or business@simonandschuster.com.

The Simon & Schuster Speakers Bureau can bring authors to your live event. For more information or to book an event, contact the Simon & Schuster Speakers Bureau at 1-866-248-3049 or visit our website at www.simonspeakers.com.

Interior design by Jaime Putorti
Illustrations by Miki Lowe

Manufactured in the United States of America

1 3 5 7 9 10 8 6 4 2

Library of Congress Control Number has been applied for.

ISBN 978-1-6682-1780-1
ISBN 978-1-6682-1781-8 (ebook)

 Let's stay in touch! Scan here to get book recommendations, exclusive offers, and more delivered to your inbox.

To my family across all the generations,
especially our beloved newest member,
Ida Camellia Williams

Contents

Introduction

If you had been at my wedding, you would remember the songs my Aunt Helen wrote for my husband and me. Months before the big day, she called up many of our friends and family members and asked them all kinds of questions about us. How did we meet? What were we like as a couple? What were some funny details about our life together? Then she wrote new lyrics to show tunes and pop songs, and secretly recruited my first cousins and some of our best friends. After the rehearsal dinner, under the tent outside an old inn with a pretty garden, they sang with gusto and goodwill, to the delight of all. There was one song about our dog, Guthrie, who would never drop a ball after she fetched it. The one about us, two history nerds who met in graduate school where we were both getting PhDs, was sung to the tune of Sam Cooke's song "Wonderful World" with its famous first line, "Don't know much about history." This was long before the time of cell phones with video cameras, so we don't have a record of that joyful, goofy tribute, but it lives on in our memories. I have a copy of the lyrics with Aunt Helen's handwritten notes tucked away in a wedding folder along with all the invitation lists and flower choices and caterer's menus. These lyrics, in their way, became a type of historical document; the songs captured details about our early lives together, and rereading them now helps us remember those as well as the hilarity of the performance itself.

The next day, at the wedding reception, you would have noticed the big, shiny metal trunk sitting on a table near the dance floor. In fact, you would have walked right up to it and deposited whatever little knickknack you'd brought with you for that very purpose. Why? Because we had asked all our wedding guests to contribute to a time capsule; we suggested you bring something you felt captured the essence of that year, 1992. At the reception, people gathered around the table, examining what other guests had donated. We loved seeing people who didn't know one another talking about why they had chosen their particular object and what future generations might think about it. The time capsule was a hit, and we were thrilled.

We raised a toast and promised to invite everyone back on our twenty-fifth wedding anniversary to open the trunk together. As young people, that seemed like eons in the future. We knew our grandparents and other elderly relatives would likely not be with us, but we would have been shocked to know some of the other friends and family who would be missing—including my beautiful, talented, creative Aunt Helen, who died tragically a few years later.

We lugged that heavy metal box around for a quarter century, from Connecticut to Wisconsin to Minnesota to North Carolina. We never looked inside. And then, as promised, we invited everyone who was still alive and whom we could still find to join us for a weekend in June of 2017 to open the time capsule. The contents turned out to be amusing: Lots and lots of stuff about Ross Perot (remember him?); a video cassette with the first episode of Jay Leno hosting *The Tonight Show*; a dog's squeaky toy in the shape of Lisa Simpson. With our dear ones around us, we pulled each piece out, one by one, and laughed or sighed about what we found. More compelling than the individual items—the pieces of historical evidence—in the metal box was the collective experience with our friends and family across time. After assembling the time capsule a generation ago, we got to experience its revelations together, remembering and reflecting, so many years later.

But that twenty-fifth-anniversary party almost didn't happen. We were torn about whether to proceed with it because our family was suffering. My beloved brother-in-law, Dan, was extremely ill with leukemia. In the end, we decided that our sadness made it all the more important to take a moment to celebrate life and love and marriage while we could—because we knew how precious they were. At the event, we paused during the toasts to raise our glasses to forty-nine-year-old Dan, who couldn't be with us. He died not long after.

During the eighteen months of Dan's illness, I felt helpless, unable to stop the slow-motion tragedy unfolding in my family. I tried to offer support around the edges; distracting my niece and nephew, cooking meals, running errands, spending long hours at the hospital, going to meetings with doctors, corralling resources, and interrogating specialists. But at a certain point, when it was clear Dan would not recover, there was only one more thing I could offer. I was a historian, after all. Devastated by the recognition that we would soon lose this generous, hilarious, brilliant, and beloved man, and determined that his wife and children would someday have the chance to hear his voice again, I asked Dan if he wanted to record an interview with me—an oral history.

By that point in my career, I'd been studying and teaching American history for decades. I'd taught at colleges and universities, written books and articles, and run programs. I had come to love the method of oral history—the practice in which historians learn about the past by interviewing people who lived through it. Listening to the life stories of people who had grown up in earlier times, hearing about their grandparents and parents, their experiences as children, their education and their careers had deeply enriched my understanding of the past and of the world around me. I was running one of the oldest oral history programs in the country, at the University of North Carolina at Chapel Hill, close to where Dan lived. To me, then, the idea of interviewing Dan felt comforting; for someone with my training, it seemed like something helpful that I could offer. I knew that, as much as I adored Dan, I had just enough emotional distance to contemplate taking on the endeavor—something his grieving wife, teenaged children, brother, and devastated parents certainly did not. But even so, I was nervous. Would the prospect feel too depressing to Dan? Would we both be overcome with emotion? Would the process do Dan and his family any good, or would it potentially cause any pain or damage?

Dan didn't hesitate, though; he readily accepted my invitation. In October of that year, a few months before he died, we sat on the couch in his living room, and for three and a half hours, he mustered the strength, both physical and emotional, to recount his life story. I remember how restless his painfully thin limbs were from the drugs he was taking; as one of his legs moved back and forth on the couch, I knew the sound of it rubbing across the upholstery would be forever captured alongside his voice. The falling leaves and darkening sky outside the window took on a kind of metaphorical significance as we talked.

I'd prepared a list of questions and guided Dan through conversations. I tried to think about both what he might want to share and what his family might want to know and remember. I wanted to give him a chance to tell people the impact they'd had on him, and what they'd meant to him, if he desired. We talked about his childhood and how his parents and his brother had influenced him, his admiration and love for them. He shared about his experiences in school, his passionate love of sports, his friendships, and his work. His memories took us to places both expected and unexpected, sometimes funny, other times serious. He grew emotional, talking about his hopes and fears for his children. I learned more about his youth and his job and his family of origin than I'd ever known. He got to spend time remembering some of the happiest and most meaningful moments in his life and to recall and recognize the people who had shaped him. When we were done, we had a digital audio file rich with his memories and the messages he wanted to be sure to pass along to his family.

When Dan passed away, the existence of this interview did little to dull his loved ones' pain. But in the very act of its creation, I think, Dan gained comfort in the knowledge that his feelings would be preserved for his family even when he was gone. The chance to reflect on his all-too-short time on earth gave him some agency to shape his story at a time when he had been robbed of other forms of power. It gifted me hours of meaningful time with a favorite relative, moments that I will treasure forever. And in time, it will offer those who loved him a way to sit with his voice again, to hear what he wanted to tell us, to get a better understanding of who he was and who he wanted to be. In the future, maybe that interview will be a way for a young person who never met Dan to learn from their grandfather or great-grandfather or second cousin once removed, and to situate themselves along the continuum of family. Together, we ensured his story lives on; and Dan's story, including his untimely death, is an incredibly important part of our story as a family.

If you are reading this book, you likely share the sense that preserving family memories is important. There might be a few reasons: Perhaps you, too, want to create a record of one life here on earth; to capture the stories and experiences of a person who is here and who has meant something to you and to others. To make sure that your family member does not go silently "into that dark night," to sort of quote Dylan Thomas, and that younger generations will get a chance to hear their voice and to know them. I hope for your sake that you are not facing the kind of untimely loss that Dan's family suffered. You might have a relative who is healthy, but elderly—you might want to interview them on the occasion of a significant birthday. Perhaps your family is moving, and you want to capture stories about your home and neighborhood before you leave. Maybe you are just curious about the past or you have a school assignment to do. (I want to note here that while I use the terms *family* and *relatives* repeatedly in this book,

I mean them expansively, to include our chosen families as well as those into which we were born. Whether or not you are related by blood or law to the people who matter most to you is of no consequence here.) No matter what, we all know that our chances to enjoy the company of our dear ones are limited.

Beyond just wanting to preserve your loved ones' voices, perhaps you recognize that their stories and experiences are profoundly important to you. We each sense intuitively that how our parents and grandparents grew up—the stories they heard from their elders, the joys and sorrows they were dealt—in turn shapes how they raised us. Many of us instinctively understand that hearing their stories—their experiences, their perspectives—might help us make sense, not just of their lives but our own.

Or you may want to go beyond one person, and piece together the story of your family more broadly. Maybe you have been drawn to genealogy, mapping out a family tree and even undertaking genetic tracing through platforms like Ancestry or 23andMe. Whether you are just getting started or have managed to find traces of your roots going back generations, you may still have more questions than answers. Birth dates, birthplaces, census and military records, marriage and death certificates—they can offer up tantalizing clues, but often, that is as far as we can get. It's easy to lose the thread in census records, for example, when a woman's name changes upon marriage. Or you might know, for instance, *when* somebody got married, but what was the relationship like? What made them laugh? Why did they decide to move from the rural area where they grew up to the city? When families have not been able to record their stories and pass them down through the generations, the historical record can be full of holes and absences. Recording your family's oral history today might help fill in some of the gaps about the past—and it can also help preserve a fuller picture of today so that future generations will benefit from this precious knowledge. Your effort today could help prevent the kinds of dead ends and looming questions that frustrate so many of us looking back. After all, as Amanda reminds us in Tennessee Williams's play *The Glass Menagerie*, "The future becomes the present, the present the past, and the past turns into everlasting regret if you don't plan for it!"

You might not think that capturing your relatives' memories is important to anyone outside your household. But as a historian, I can tell you that your work to record your own family history could potentially help those of us who are professionals in years to come. As we seek to tell a full, rich, complex history of the nation, we need to understand how individuals and families experienced change over time. How did 9/11 reshape the way we thought about our country, our safety, our place in the world? How did the rise of cell phones and social media change the experiences of childhood and parenting? What was the impact of the COVID pandemic on families and communities? Since fewer and fewer people are writing letters and keeping diaries—some of the key ways we historians used to learn about the experiences of everyday people in the past—we need to be sure to create new kinds of records. Historians in the future will need creative ways to understand those of us living today. Reviewing social media feeds might be one way they do it. But how revealing will those be of our deepest thoughts and observations? If you capture your families' stories, experiences, and reflections on the world today and preserve them, you could help future historians understand one piece of this complex puzzle we call America.

I hope that in *Our Story,* you find the encouragement you need and the guidance you want to take a joyful and creative approach to family history, with interviewing at the core. There are plenty of guides available to help you search the archives for genealogical clues to your family's long-ago past and document your family tree. I encourage you to make use of those resources—you can find some in the additional reading section of this book. My approach here, however, is focused on seeking a deeper understanding of the more recent past from those who are still living, by asking them about their experiences and memories. In this approach, while you might start with ancestry platforms or in historical societies and library archives, the goal is to get together and talk. Here, just as important as collecting facts and dates is having meaningful conversations, often across generations. The conversations can be as in-depth or as lighthearted as you wish. I suggest prompts in this book, but once you get the idea, you'll probably come up with more on your own that fit the particular circumstances of your unique family.

Professional historians use oral history techniques to learn about all kinds of things—what it was like to live and work in a particular factory town, for example, or to experience the women's movement in the 1970s, or to start a new business as a recent immigrant to Atlanta in the 1990s. Their interviews are recorded, usually transcribed, and preserved for future generations. Because they have saved those interviews for many decades in archives around the country, we can hear voices from very long ago—women talking about what it was like to fight for the right to vote, or men remembering what it felt like to fight in World War II, or how life changed when electricity arrived in their town. The experiences of everyday, regular people constitute history; even if we have not been "leaders" in our communities or been the catalyst for major changes in society, all of us have both contributed to and experienced change over time.

I hope that notion gives you the confidence you need to start your own project. Because people often think that history happened long ago and far away to people not like them. But it is the decisions and actions of people just like you and those in your family and your neighborhood that constitute so much of our nation's history. Presidents and politicians and military leaders and business leaders make many important decisions that impact the rest of us—and in very traditional views of history, their actions were all that mattered. But not anymore. How we respond is also the stuff of history. How did your family make it through the Depression, and how did that shape their beliefs about work, poverty, or the government? Did anyone in your family serve in a war, and how did that change the trajectory of their lives? How did your family experience the Jim Crow era and the legal challenges to it? How did your grandmother and mother feel about the expectations of women in their time, and what messages did they pass along about those ideas? All of us have stories worth hearing, sharing, and saving.

Your work will be important. Whether your family came to America within the last generation or hundreds of years ago; whether they came willingly or under duress; whether they have flourished on American soil or struggled; whether they lived through the civil rights movement, fought in Vietnam, or watched the towers fall on September 11. By documenting and preserving your family's experiences, not only can you better understand how and why you and your family have developed the way you have but you are helping to build the historical record that allows us to better understand how our country has developed the way it has.

You may plan to share your family history with just your own circle, or you may hope to share it more widely; in either case, *Our Story* will give you plenty of step-by-step guidance on how to carry out your project from start to finish. It is packed with practical suggestions and creative approaches, and I hope it will be one you can rely on and return to again and again as you undertake this thrilling project.

I commend you for committing to this effort. Whether you plan to have a conversation with one beloved family member or are contemplating how to gather the recollections of many loved ones, oral history interviews can be a powerful and important experience, both for the interviewer and for the person being interviewed. How often do we get the chance in our daily lives to listen, deeply and attentively, to the life experiences of another person? To follow our curiosity and learn about the details of their childhood pastimes or their teenage romances or first jobs? How often do they have the chance to share at length about what they've learned from life, to pass on memories that have stuck with them for decades, confess to dreams deferred or mistakes made or wishes unfulfilled, or to express pride in what they accomplished? To listen deeply and at length to another person's story can be a profoundly moving experience. To be listened to, with respect and curiosity and patience, is for many people an unfortunately rare occurrence—and one that often means the world.

The first part of this book offers suggestions for things to consider before you start gathering your family together to share their stories or sitting down with your grandmother to interview her. While you can certainly just dive in to talking with your relatives, your project will probably benefit from some preparatory efforts. We will explore how your motivation for undertaking the project and what you hope the result will be should shape your approach. I'll review how making certain choices ahead of time can prevent frustration down the road when you are putting together your final product. And I'll give a brief overview of the kinds of background research you might consider undertaking before you start your first interview.

The second part of the book will help set you up for success during the interviews themselves. From thinking through when and where to do your interviews, to what kinds of recording devices (if any) to use, to types of topics you might explore, to suggestions for questions you could ask, this part will help you feel confident. You'll get some ideas for creative ways you might approach the interviewing experience, and helpful suggestions for what to do when challenging moments arise, like trying to interview a forgetful grandparent or a taciturn uncle.

In the third part of the book, we'll cover what to do once the interviews are over. How will you compile your research and share it with others? We'll consider whether to transcribe your interviews and what options there are for how to do that. If you are thinking about writing up your research into a family history book or article, you'll find suggestions for ways to organize the information and present the richness of the stories you've discovered. And we'll go over different options for how to share the results of your project, whether in written form or other potential formats.

In the additional reading section, you'll find suggestions for further reading and other resources to help you along the way. You'll see throughout a series of questions for you to consider and space to jot down your answers. Go ahead—write in the book! My hope is that by thinking through these questions as you go, by the time you reach the end you'll feel ready!

No matter why you are reading this book, I hope you will find in it what you need to help you begin to explore your family's history. As a historian who has been studying the past for over three decades now, I am passionate about helping people recognize how the past shapes the way we see the present. One excellent step in that direction is by understanding how our own family's story shapes our experiences and our outlook today. For instance, your grandfather's attitude toward immigrants may be shaped by how he reflects on his own parents' immigration story. Asking him about that past and how he reflects on it may help you understand him.

Moreover, history can also strengthen our empathy, not just for our own families but also for others, no matter how similar or different they may seem. Maybe your white great-uncle went to college or bought his first house with help from the GI Bill after World War II, for instance. How infuriating might it have been for your brother-in-law's grandfather if, as a Black soldier returning from the same war, he was not able to enjoy those same benefits? Learning our families' stories and understanding how they have been shaped by the broader social, legal, and political contexts helps us see connections to the history of our country and to all its inhabitants. By starting with the inner concentric circle of our own family's history, I also hope that we can begin to recognize how our family's story fits into that of our neighborhood, our hometown, our nation.

Whatever the result of your undertaking, I hope you and your loved ones will celebrate and enjoy the process of learning together. By seeking to preserve these family stories now, I hope you will grow closer to your loved ones while they are still alive. In gathering to listen deeply to our relatives' stories and their interpretations of the past, we gain a fuller understanding of them, our families, ourselves, and those around us. No matter which route you take, the journey of gathering stories will provide you rich, meaningful time with your relatives. The history you are preserving is for the generations to follow. The collaborative making of the history is for you and your loved ones, now.

Part One

Before the Interviews

My father's mother was born in Ukraine in 1896. When she came to the United States with my grandfather in 1922, she spoke only Yiddish. My father translated for her throughout his childhood. He went away for college and started to work as a high school English teacher near Boston, but he came back home to Cleveland to care for her when she was bedridden with congestive heart failure. She died at age sixty-six, and my father realized he'd never really asked her about her early life.

My grandfather lived much longer, and my father did try to ask him about life in the old country. But Grandpa Phil didn't want to talk about it. "We were poor," he would always say. "We had nothing. America is the best country. Why do you want to know?" For decades, my father was frustrated but accepted that he simply would never learn much about his parents' life in eastern Europe.

But there was one story my grandfather would share, and it became the central piece of our family's lore. I heard it repeatedly as a child from my father and his siblings. It was the story of my grandfather leaving his homeland and meeting my grandmother along the way.

The story, as I heard it with a child's ears, was like a fairy tale. I remember hearing that my grandfather decided to leave Proskurov, Ukraine, on foot. It was 1919, not long after World War I had ended, and he was supposedly running from the Russian army, because conscription for a young Jewish soldier would likely have meant years of suffering and indignities at the hands of antisemitic military officers. When he stopped to rest in a nearby village, he heard a young woman crying. In some versions of the story, at least in my memory, he actually came upon her on the banks of a frozen river, where her evil stepmother forced her to wash the family's clothes. "If you have compassion in your heart, take me with you," the young woman said when he went over to talk to her. A week later, they were married and left the village; eventually, they made it to the United States and then to Cleveland, where her sister already lived. When I was a child, it was a romantic tale; as I got older, I heard the desperation in my grandmother's request.

In 2012, long after my grandparents had died, my first cousin and his wife traveled in the opposite direction, from Cleveland back to Proskurov, Ukraine, to see the site of our family's origin story. They found there the remnants of a mass grave and a memorial to more than a thousand Jews who had been murdered in a single day in 1919 in a horrifying pogrom. Neither Grandpa Phil nor my Grandmother Fanny, who died before I was born, had ever mentioned this event. Suddenly, the context for my grandfather's decision to leave his hometown was terrifyingly illuminated. Is that the real reason he left? Had he witnessed the atrocities? Did he know people who were killed? Even if it happened after he'd moved, would that explain why he never wanted to talk about his homeland?

My cousins' trip was a turning point for my father, who kept thinking about his parents' past in a new way. The discovery of that momentous piece of information, and the desire to learn more about the fuller picture of his parents' lives, led him to embark on a multiyear research and writing project. He read about the history of Jews in Ukraine, and the impact of World War I. He studied maps and went to genealogy conferences; he talked to librarians and scholars who helped him track down details about where his parents had lived and translated Russian documents for him.

But my father's favorite part of the undertaking was talking with family members near and far about what they had heard, what stories had been passed down to them. (I should note here that my father wrote his own book on interviewing as a research methodology—I learned from the best!) Though my grandparents had died, there were other relatives with whom he could speak. He talked with those he knew in the United States and also reached out to some as far away as Israel and Canada, by email and telephone. "I wonder if your parents ever told you any stories about my parents?" he asked. They shared what they could, and sometimes the stories were illuminating. My father already knew that his father had started out in Cleveland as a peddler, selling small goods from a cart on the city streets, until over time, he opened a furniture store. But now he learned how Phil had become a salesman as a child back in Ukraine. A girl cousin, a few years older than he was, had taken pity when he showed up without shoes one day. She got him started with a sack of flour and taught him the basics of how to make a profit by selling to people in the neighborhood—passing along to him the skills that would sustain him and his family for decades.

Another cousin told my father a harrowing story that, although not directly about Phil or Fanny, added to his understanding of the violence and lawlessness from which his parents were escaping. Fanny's half-brother Shike was a teenager in 1919 when Cossacks came into his village. Many decades later, Shike's son told my father how they had forced all the Jews into the center of the village and surrounded them on horseback. When one soldier pointed to Shike's shoes, he immediately took them off and handed them over. But his friend, who was standing next to him, hesitated. The soldier leaned down from his saddle and slashed the boy's neck with his sword, killing him instantly. That night, Shike's mother gave him money and sent him away from home forever, hidden under hay in a wagon.

My father was grateful to hear new pieces of the story from these family members, and to find new perspectives from which to understand his parents' relationships to each other and to others in their community. As he told me later, though, the most meaningful part was the simple act of talking with his relatives and relishing a new sense of connection through the collaborative piecing together of their family story. He spent two years on the project, and in 2014, in his mid-seventies, he self-published *So You Might Know: A Memoir of My Parents.*

My father was motivated by a variety of complicated emotions—yearning to comprehend his parents, guilt over lost opportunities to ask them questions, a sense that others could help him understand his family, and even, therefore, himself. As a teacher, scholar, and expert interviewer, my father hoped that this research would bring him a deeper understanding of and connection to his parents, and a way to pass on to his children and grandchildren a fuller picture of our family's story. He found himself energized, engaged, and deeply committed to the process of researching and writing. Although he was the driving force behind the project, it became a collective endeavor—my mother, who is an archivist, provided constant support and advice; other people shared photographs, documents, and reminiscences that my father included. As he was wrapping up, he asked each of Phil and Fanny's grandchildren, including me, to send in our memories of them to be woven into the story. The result is a book that captures as much of that side of our family's history as is available and that will be passed on to generations from now on. My father's experience writing it—and the many lessons he has passed on to me over the decades before and since—have shaped my own approach to this book. It was a project that, after all, drew on all types of history-making—including oral history methods.

 *Creating a Project Road Map*

You may be like my father; you, too, may thrill to the idea of a yearslong project with in-depth background research, talking to many different people, and writing a book. But perhaps that sounds like far too much work and not at all what you had in mind—you might be hoping for a much simpler project and just want some guidance on how to ask family members some good questions. Perhaps you are not sure yet—maybe you just want to get started and see where it leads you. These are all perfectly reasonable mindsets!

In this section of the book, I suggest some things you may want to think about before you jump in, because they might help you as your project unfolds. Think of this phase like planning a road trip—by taking time to mull over a few key decisions, you can map out a fun and productive route and still leave plenty of room for serendipitous discovery along the way. For instance, if you were planning a trip, you'd probably want to identify what you're hoping for. Do you want to get as far as you can as fast as possible? Major highways are for you.

But if your hope is to meander along at a leisurely rate, stopping in small towns and getting a sense of how locals live in the areas you're traversing, then scenic byways and backroads are the way to go.

How far? Does it matter if you get all the way across the country, or will you be satisfied by seeing one beautiful new place? You'd probably also want to consider who is going with you. Are you on your own? Or do you have traveling companions? Will you have a bunch of young kids in the car? That might affect how many hours per day you drive, and what sights you seek out along the way. And what kind of car do you have? If you don't have all-wheel drive, maybe it's not such a good idea to drive across Montana in the winter, and you'd be better off going through the South. Finally, are you an old soul, happy just to have the experience for yourself and your companions IRL, or do you feel compelled to share your trip's sights and highlights with others? If so, you can use your cell phone and social media, or you might want to pack your camera, or maybe an easel with watercolors, or your journal and favorite pen. If you're going to want to make a movie, don't forget to take videos along the way.

Likewise, when planning a family history undertaking, thinking through a few key questions up front can help you set yourself up for success in researching and telling your family's story.

In this section of the book, we'll go over a checklist of items for you to consider before you start researching your family story.

* Motivation
* Audience
* Scope
* Resources
* Format

Of course, sometimes we just hop in the car and hit the road. None of what follows is prescriptive; there are probably as many ways to undertake a family history as there are families. Take what is useful and ignore what feels like it will get in your way.

Motivation

If you can identify WHY you want to take on this project, you're more likely to set up a process that will help you feel satisfied with the results.

For example, if you simply are curious about your own parents' experiences and want the chance to talk with them at length while they are still with you, you can jump to part 2 of this book, where I give you some suggestions for topics to consider and questions to ask. You don't even need to record the interviews—for you, maybe the chance to sit together, ask questions, and listen deeply is enough. Especially if you think your opportunities for this kind of connection are limited— maybe you don't see them often, or they are very elderly, or perhaps they are starting to lose their memories—then taking the extra time to do background research is not necessary and might even prevent you from reaching your main goal. Like a leisurely Sunday drive through beautiful landscapes, the project, in your case, consists of the process. Your satisfaction will come from expressing interest in their experiences, planning some questions ahead of time, and making room in your busy life to sit and listen to their answers. Here, the connection through sharing stories is the main thing, and that is enough.

Maybe you know quite a lot about your parents' lives, and you are most interested in trying to understand the life of someone else in your family—perhaps the matriarch of the family or a quirky uncle—who has always been a bit of a mystery to you and who is no longer around. Maybe you sense that there is a reason nobody talks about them much, and you feel that the silences are significant. In this case, there is a particular destination in mind, and mapping out a route makes some sense, because if you don't get those questions answered, you may feel frustrated. You could do background research to find out as much as possible about your relative from the historical record and then interview family members to fill in the details, learn what you can about their personalities, and find out about how they impacted those around them. You could ask directly about why there seems to be some secrecy around their story, or you could try to interpret the answer from what people do and don't say. The section in this part on background research will help you consider where to start before you jump into interviewing others, and in part 2, I share some tips that may come in handy on how to deal with tricky situations and ethical dilemmas if you're investigating this kind of family mystery.

Perhaps you are motivated by the idea of capturing as much as possible about your family as a whole, rather than just insights into one or two people. And you may feel it's important to preserve the stories you hear and the knowledge you gain and to share them with others in a way that will do justice to the stories and capture your audience's attention. Just like with a long, cross-country road trip, careful planning will help prevent wrong turns. You'll want to think through not just how to do background research and how to interview people but how to present your research in compelling ways. For you, part 3, in which I suggest even more ideas for how to compile and share your family stories, will be useful.

Here is a list of potential motivations. Does one of these speak to you? Or do you sense that there is a different reason behind your desire to dive into family history?

* Wanting to capture the stories of aging family members before it's too late
* Feeling curious about the past and your family's experiences
* Wondering how your family got to be the way that it is
* Wondering how you got to be the way that you are
* Wanting to document achievements and celebrate successes
* Needing a way to grapple with family losses and commemorate loved ones
* Seeking to overcome silences and taboo topics
* Settling debates or disagreements about what really happened in the past
* Desiring to educate younger generations about the experiences of their elders and ancestors
* Hoping for increased connection and understanding among family members
* Looking to initiate new family traditions
* Wanting to create meaningful gifts for momentous occasions
* Needing a focus for your intellectual and creative energies

My Motivation:

Why do I want to do this?

_____

_____

_____

_____

_____

_____

Is there a specific goal I'm hoping to achieve?

_____

_____

_____

_____

_____

Which particular people or stories interest me?

_____

_____

_____

_____

_____

_____

What questions have I always had about my family history?

_____

_____

_____

_____

_____

_____

Am I motivated by learning the history, or am I most interested in the process itself, and connecting with people who are alive in the moment?

_____

_____

_____

_____

_____

Am I excited or nervous about doing background research?

_____

_____

_____

_____

_____

_____

How much do I care about creating a final product that can be shared with others?

_____

_____

_____

_____

_____

_____

Audience

When we moved from Minnesota to North Carolina with our two daughters, aged seven and ten, my husband and I mapped out a route that had us driving five hours per day for five days, with enough time to stop in towns and cities along the way, see a friend here and there, and take in some kid-friendly sights. If it had just been the two of us, we probably would have tried to get to our new home more quickly. But for this trip to be successful, we had to combine our motivations with the kids' needs. Similarly, when undertaking a project like this, it helps to think about your intended audience as though they are your traveling companions. Even though you might be the driver of the project, knowing whom you want to share your story with can shape how you approach your research, your interviews, and your final product.

When I start a new historical research project, I ask myself whether I am hoping to share this with young students, adult learners, or experts. No matter how interested I am in a particular topic, I need to consider things like how old my audience is, what their reading or comprehension level is, how much background knowledge they already have, and how much interest they have in the topic to effectively do my job.

You, too, might want to think about your audience as you plan your research approach, your interviews, and your final product. With whom do you imagine sharing this? Children, adults, or both? Family members only, or others in your community or beyond? People who love to read, or people who might prefer other ways of learning?

If Your Audience Members Are Children

How do you want to focus your project so that you convey the history you want but in a way that is of interest to kids? A few ideas to consider: One is to focus your interviews on what it was like for your family members when they were children. You could ask questions about the material realities of their lives—young children today would probably be fascinated by stories of telephones stuck to the wall and how we used to look up phone numbers in a big book that we also sat on when the table was too high, or how we cut out pictures from the Sears catalog when we were stuck at home, sick in bed. The following are just a few suggestions of questions that might yield stories that would interest children. You could also involve children in your family in coming up with the questions to ask.

* What do you remember about your family home growing up?
* What were your favorite rooms in the house and why?
* Paint the scene for me when you came home after school: Who would we see there? What might we have smelled coming from the kitchen? What sounds might we have heard?
* What chores did you have to do, and how did you feel about them?
* Were chores the same for your siblings, or did girls and boys have different tasks to do?
* Did you get an allowance? What did you do with your money? How did your family talk about spending, saving, and giving away money?
* Who were your closest friends, and what did you like to do together?
* How do you think your friends would have described you as a child?

* What was your favorite toy or game?
* What do you remember about your childhood pets?
* Where did you go to school, and how would you describe yourself as a student?
* What did you like most and least about school?
* Were there any teachers who had a particularly important impact on you?
* What do you think are the biggest differences between your childhood and those of kids today?
* What was your favorite holiday to celebrate with your family as a child?
* What traditions did you practice then that you don't practice now, and which ones did you carry on?
* Tell me about a great family trip you took in childhood—what do you remember best?
* What were some of your favorite childhood meals?
* Do you have a particular memory from childhood that stands out to you?

See part 2 for more ideas on topics to consider and questions to ask.

If Your Audience Members Are Adults

If your intended audience is adults, your approach might be somewhat different. With adults in mind, you might include more emphasis on your interviewees' experiences of work, romance, marriage, child-rearing, and the like. You might be more likely to tackle complex issues, like your family's attitudes toward money and social class, or immigration, or racial dynamics in your town or within your own family. You might ask about participation in military service or social movements. Perhaps there are stories in your family's past that you would not want to focus on with children as the audience but that adults in the family would be ready to hear.

Topics you might address with adult audiences in mind (again, see part 2 for more ideas):

* How would you describe dating culture when you were in high school?
* What were your own early experiences with romance like?
* Did you go to college, and why or why not?
* What were you expecting from college, and how did your experiences at school match up or not?
* Who were important friends, teachers, advisors, or mentors you had as a young adult, and how did they shape you?
* What were your expectations, if any, for marriage and family life and how did your experiences compare to what you imagined?
* What do you remember about your first job?

* What did you do with your first paycheck, and how did you feel about it?

* Where were you when 9/11 (or another major historical event) happened? What do you remember about that day, and how did that experience shape you?

* What impact do you think that event had on your family, your town, or the country?

* How did COVID affect you and your family?

* What do you think you will remember most about the early days of the pandemic?

* What have been your experiences with illness in your family?

* How has receiving care or providing care to loved ones affected you?

* Have there been important moments of loss in your life? How have you handled grief, and what impact have the losses had on you and the wider family?

Family Only or Non-Family Members?

For most of us, the audience we have in mind when we undertake researching our family's history is other family members. In some cases, though, your family's story may be of interest to others outside your kin. Perhaps your grandfather, for instance, founded a beloved hardware store and played an important civic role in your town; the local historical society might relish a copy of his interview. Or maybe your cousin helped start a storefront church that is still going strong; generations of congregants might be intrigued by that origin story. Or your great-grandmother's experiences as a Rosie the Riveter during World War II could help students at the local middle school understand the impact of the war on the home front, and the social studies teachers would be grateful to you for sharing the information.

If your audience might include people who are outside your family, then that might require a slightly different approach. For instance, you may need to be more explicit about certain things that, if you were sharing only with family members, might go unspoken. You can't assume that everybody will know who your family members are or how they are connected—you'll need to explain things more clearly for external audiences. Inside jokes and knowing asides won't be as clear to external audiences, so if you want them to understand, you may have to explain.

If you are going to share with public audiences, considerations of privacy also come into play in new ways—there might be some stories that your interviewees wouldn't want you to share with those who are not family; you will want to think ahead about getting permission to use people's interviews for audiences that might include strangers.

In part 2, we'll talk more about these issues and provide some more examples.

My Audience:

For whom do I want to do this?

_____

_____

_____

_____

_____

Who is my primary audience–children, adults, or both?

_____

_____

_____

_____

_____

_____

Who else might be interested in my family's history and why?

_____

_____

_____

_____

_____

_____

What are some ways that my intended audience might shape how I think about my project?

_____

_____

_____

_____

_____

_____

Scope

It's worth thinking ahead about the scope of this project. How will you define the beginning and end? How will you know when you are done?

You might start by thinking about how far back you want to try to trace your family. For genealogists, there is a great deal of interest and excitement in going back as far as you can, using creative approaches to background research in things like marriage and death certificates, military records, immigration records, census records, and so on. Because this book is especially about the use of oral history, our focus is on the more recent past—the past that people can remember or the stories they've heard and can pass along. So, for instance, you might say to yourself that you are focused on telling the story of your family over the last fifty to seventy-five years. This can be one piece of a bigger project with a longer scope—combining genealogical approaches with this oral history approach—or it can be a stand-alone project.

There are other questions besides the time period you'll try to cover. How big a project are you undertaking?

* Do you want to focus on just one or two people?
* On a specific generation?
* A specific subgroup, like the women in your family, or the veterans?

* The family members who live in a particular town or region?

* A particular "branch" of the family, or the whole kit and caboodle?

There are lots of different ways to define the scope of your project. It's good to start with an idea, at least; it may change over time as you go.

My Scope:

How do I want to define the chronological scope of this project?

_____

_____

_____

_____

_____

What is the scope of the project in terms of a particular generation, topic, or theme?

_____

_____

_____

_____

_____

Whom would this lead me to include, and whom might it mean I leave out?

_____

_____

_____

_____

_____

_____

Are there particular people I'm interested in knowing more about?

_____

_____

_____

_____

_____

If those people aren't alive or available to interview, who might know more about them?

_____

_____

_____

_____

_____

_____

Resources

What you have in terms of time, money, and talents will shape how you approach this project. Perhaps you are retired and this project can constitute a central focus of your attention for as long as it takes. On the other hand, maybe you are a working mother and you want to define a project that could be finished in time for your parents' fiftieth wedding anniversary, which is happening next month. Perhaps you are able to invest significant funds into traveling a long distance to interview relatives. But if travel is difficult for you, or you need to stick to a shoestring budget, then you might include only local family members or use Zoom or other online platforms for recording. Your own talents will guide you as well; if you are a digital native, editing audio online may be relatively easy for you, and developing a podcast would be a fun challenge; for others, learning to upload an MP3 might be more than enough tech for the day and you want to stick to a text-based project like editing interview transcripts. Whether you have others interested in helping you—like an artistic daughter who could illustrate your work with pen-and-ink drawings or a nephew who could help you gather photographs from family members—can also make a difference. And there is also your community and the resources you have available there; maybe you have a great public library with a particularly strong local history branch or perhaps an enthusiastic genealogist neighbor who can introduce you to some online databases. Taking stock of your resources is a good idea as you define your project.

My Resources:

How much time do I have for this?

_____

_____

_____

_____

How much money do I have for this?

_____

_____

_____

_____

What talents can I draw on for this?

_____

_____

_____

_____

_____

_____

Who else might want to help me, and what might they contribute?

_____

_____

_____

_____

_____

_____

Format

Once you've thought about your motivation, your audience, your scope, and your resources, you might start to formulate some ideas about how you are going to compile and present your research when it is complete.

I always try to start by imagining my audience (refer to the earlier section for more on that!). Then I ask three questions:

* What do I want to share?
* What do they want (or need) to learn?
* What do I want their experience to be?

The answers to these questions help you determine what format will work best.

As a professor and a museum curator, I have used many different formats to share historical research, including lectures, books, articles, exhibitions, digital projects, podcasts, op-eds, blogs, and online essays. As a family historian, you have even more freedom to think about creative and fun formats that will help you satisfy your own motivations and meet the needs of your audiences!

If I wanted to write about an important but under-recognized figure in history and my imagined audience was fourth graders, maybe I would team up with an artist to create a graphic novel depicting her life; if I were writing about the same person for adult audiences, I'd probably choose a different format. If I'm going to give a talk to a conference of professional historians, my approach will be different than if I'm speaking in front of a local community group.

So what will you do? You might be like my father, with a lot of time, energy, and writing skills, so perhaps you want to write a book and self-publish it. You like the idea that it can be referred to over and over and will live on family bookshelves. But there are lots of other ways to go! The format need not be anything like a book. You could write a play about your family, or even a musical, and perform it at an event, like my Aunt Helen's wedding gift to us. Or, if you're artistically talented, you could represent what you learned through paintings, drawings, or other creative means. The following are some ideas to get you started thinking. But there are even more ideas, with practical advice about how to make them a reality, later in this book. For now, ask yourself: Which ones interest you, and which ones do you think meet your own goals plus your audiences' needs?

You don't have to decide now—and you can always change your mind—but again, it's useful to at least think about your desired final project at the beginning, because it might shape how you conduct your interviews and research. If you know you want to create a documentary film, for instance, it's probably a good idea to videotape the interviews. On the other hand, if you want to make a podcast, you don't need video; you could just use audio recordings. In either case, you'd probably want transcriptions of your interviews, which will make it much easier, for instance, to find the highlights you want to feature. We will go into more detail on how to do your interviews in part 2 and how to plan potential final products in part 3.

Here is a short list of formats to get you thinking about what's possible for your project; consider which ones of these might be a good fit for your own motivation, audience, scope, and resources:

* Create a picture book, illustrating one memory for each family member with whimsical drawings. Or leave the pages blank and ask the children to draw a picture to go with the story.
* Write a play that can be performed by family members at a holiday gathering.
* Write songs for the whole family to sing that capture some key family moments.
* Compile a collection of transcripts of the interviews, with photographs to illustrate the stories, and brief introductions that you write, putting the interviews into context.
* Edit clips of videotaped interviews with old family photographs into a documentary film.
* Record a podcast using clips from the interviews, perhaps with episodes for each person, or for themes that

pull from different people's lives (such as an episode on food, an episode on work, an episode on funny family moments . . .).

* Host a potluck dinner, in which each person brings a dish with a story to go along with it (who taught them to make it, who it reminds them of, when they used to eat it, why it's important to them . . .), and then you compile the stories and recipes into a book.

* Design a science-fair-style poster exhibit that you set up on a table at your next family gathering.

* Write a self-published memoir.

* Get the teenagers in your family to write a set of poems based on the memories shared in the interviews.

My (Potential) Format

My first thoughts on a final product:

_____

_____

_____

_____

_____

_____

Which of the above formats appeal most to me?

_____

_____

_____

_____

_____

_____

How do they fit with my motivation, audience, resources, and scope?

_____

_____

_____

_____

Do I have a different idea that might work?

_____

_____

_____

_____

_____

_____

Why might that be better?

_____

_____

_____

_____

_____

_____

If I were to do that final project, what should I consider while doing my research and interviews?

_____

_____

_____

_____

_____

_____

Audio or video?

_____

_____

_____

_____

_____

Other considerations?

_____

_____

_____

_____

_____

Is this format realistic for me given the time and resources I have? Do I have a backup plan?

_____

_____

_____

_____

_____

 *Background Research*

WHY to Do Research

Now that you have considered your motivations, your audience, your scope, your resources, and your potential final product, you can determine your approach to background research.

Why do background research? Why not just start talking to people?

Well, when you plan a trip, do you like to research the towns you'll be going to? Do you dig up articles about the history of the area, or reviews of the top ten restaurants, and write down lists of can't-miss sights? Maybe you go to the library and ask for help finding a novel set in the region you'll be driving through, or you choose a podcast for the road that connects to your destination. These are all ways of doing background research for your trip. They are not absolutely necessary steps to take, but they probably add richness to your experience. They help by giving you some context for what you notice as you enter new places, and they provide some ways to connect to the unfamiliar.

Of course, some people just like to arrive at a new place and experience it fresh, talking to locals and soaking up what they can about the area. Likewise, you don't have to do background research before you start interviewing your family members. But in many cases, it might deepen your pleasure and help you craft an interview experience that will be enjoyable in the moment and satisfying afterward.

While you can do your interviews first and then do research to help you fill in gaps or to explain things you aren't sure you understand, I recommend starting with at least a little bit of research first. This will help you understand the time period in which your family's stories took place. Every person and every family is unique, and we all make decisions for many different reasons, but our choices have been shaped by forces outside of our own homes; for instance, by political changes, legal turning points, or social movements. Reading about these events ahead of time could help you understand the broader context in which your family members were living, and that will make you a better interviewer.

Background research can also give you some great ideas for questions to ask. You might discover information about something specific you'd like to investigate. When my father saw the ship manifest with his parents' names on it, he was surprised to see my grandfather listed as a shoemaker. Grandpa Phil was not, in fact, a shoemaker. So that raised some interesting questions for my father to ask his family members! Why would Grandpa Phil have said that? Did anybody know if he ever made shoes? No one had a perfect answer, but it was a great avenue for conversation.

Reading more generally about the time period your family member lived in can help you formulate some questions. For instance, if you know your family member lived through World War II, you might want to read about life in the United States during the 1940s and '50s. You'd learn, for instance, about the impact of new legislation like the 1944 GI Bill, which provided many veterans with funds for college education and access to low-interest mortgages. That, in turn, led to a swift rise in the middle class and the rapid expansion of suburbs, dramatically changing the contours of many families' lives. Reading about these changes might prompt you to ask how many of your family members were veterans and if the GI Bill changed their access to college educations or their ability to get a loan for a house.

That time period also witnessed decades of the Great Migration, when many Black families left the South in search of better jobs and a more hospitable life in the North. Their journeys reshaped communities both in the South and in the North, forever changing the outlines of many families' stories. Reading about this history might prompt you to ask about how these shifts affected your own families; you might ask why they left home, what they hoped to find in their new community, and how their dreams were answered, or not. If your family already lived in the North, you might ask about whether they noticed the changes in their communities and how that played out in their own lives. Or if your family, white or Black, stayed in the South, you might ask how their lives or their community changed due to the Great Migration.

Or your background readings about this same period might discuss how, despite all the gratitude expressed to Rosie the Riveters during World War II, afterward women were encouraged to leave the workforce to make room for returning soldiers and focus their attention on raising children. Some of it was direct—like factories firing women so they could hire men—but some of it was more indirect, communicated through popular culture. Take a look at advertisements and TV shows from the time period, like *Leave It to Beaver.* If you think that might be relevant to your family member, you could jot down a note to ask how they felt about that. Perhaps something like: "Mom, I found this ad for a vacuum cleaner from the 1950s. Looking back, how do you think your expectations about marriage and family life were shaped by things like this in the 1950s? Do you remember any one piece of popular culture that had a particularly strong impact on how you imagined your own life?"

In part 2, we'll go into more detail about potential questions to ask during your interviews; I just wanted to show, here, how background research will help you enrich this process.

In addition to helping you come up with your interview

questions, doing background research will also help you understand the context for the answers you hear (or don't hear).
After my cousin told my father about his trip to Ukraine and
how he saw the memorial for victims of the pogrom in our
grandfather's hometown, my father read about life for Jews in
Ukraine in the years after World War I and got a better sense
of the political and social situation surrounding his father's escape. It helped him understand why his father hadn't wanted
to talk about the past. It explained some of the silences he'd
grown up with and motivated him to learn more from other
family members.

Having a sense of the historical period in which your family
member lived can give you more insight into the particulari-
ties of their experience and the lives of others whose families
are different from yours. If you've read about redlining and
how Black veterans did not, in practice, get the same access
to the GI Bill mortgages as white veterans due to discrimi-
natory bank lending practices, it might help you understand
your neighborhood and others in your hometown. Many
Japanese-Americans who were confined to internment camps
during World War II avoided speaking about that trauma
with their families. With research under your belt, you might
ask your aunt how she spent her time during those long days
and years and how it shaped her perspective on this country
afterward.

What to Research

The following is a partial list of major turning points, events, and social movements of the last one hundred years—times that might be within the memory of those you are interviewing or about which they might have heard stories from their elders. I've listed these in roughly chronological order. You can use this list to think about which ones might be relevant to your family's experience and which ones you might want to research more. You can add your own ideas to this list as well!

Selected List of Important Turning Points, Events, Social Movements, Inventions within Living Memory

1929–1939: The Great Depression

1933–1945: Franklin Roosevelt administration and the New Deal

1939–1945: World War II and the home front

1945–1953: Harry Truman administration

1940s and '50s: The McCarthy Era

1950–1953: Korean War

1953–1961: Dwight Eisenhower administration

1954: *Brown v. Board of Education*

1955: Polio vaccine developed

1955: Murder of Emmett Till

1950s and 1960s: Civil rights movement

1960: John F. Kennedy elected president

1960: Birth control pill approved

1963: Assassination of John F. Kennedy

1963–1969: Lyndon Johnson administration and the Great Society

1964: Civil Rights Act passed

1965: Voting Rights Act passed

1965: Immigration and Nationality Act signed

1965–1970: Delano grape strike

1965–1975: Vietnam War and anti–Vietnam War movement

1965–late 1960s: Black power movement

1966: Founding of National Organization for Women

1960s: Counterculture

1968: Assassinations of Martin Luther King Jr. and Robert F. Kennedy

1969–1974: Richard Nixon administration

1969: Neil Armstrong moon landing

1972–1974: Watergate scandal

1972: *Roe v. Wade* legalizes abortion and Title IX signed into law

1974: Equal Credit Opportunity Act passes, giving women ability to access credit in their own name

1974–1977: Gerald Ford administration

1977–1981: Jimmy Carter administration

1970s: Energy crisis

1981–1989: Ronald Reagan administration

1983: First commercially available handheld mobile phone

1986: Launch and explosion of Space Shuttle *Challenger*

1980s–1990s: Rise of the New Right

1980s: AIDS crisis

1980s: Home computers enter market

1989–1993: George H. W. Bush administration

1990: Americans with Disabilities Act signed

1993–2001: Bill Clinton administration

1994: North American Free Trade Agreement takes effect

1995: Oklahoma City bombing

1998: Google launches

2001–2009: George W. Bush administration

2001: September 11 terrorist attacks

2005: First video uploaded to YouTube

2005: Hurricane Katrina

2007–2009: The Great Recession

2007: Introduction of Apple iPhone

2009–2016: Barack Obama administration; first African American president

2015: Legalization of same-sex marriage (*Obergefell v. Hodges*)

2016: First woman nominated by Democratic Party for president: Hillary Clinton

2017–2021: First Donald Trump administration

2017: #MeToo movement emerges

2020: COVID-19 pandemic begins

2020: Protests for racial equity and against police brutality following death of George Floyd

2021–2025: Joe Biden administration

2021: Supporters of Donald Trump attack the United States Capitol on January 6

2022: Launch of ChatGPT

2024: Donald Trump elected second time

List of turning point moments that seem relevant to my family:

_____

_____

_____

_____

_____

Other important moments not included on the list but relevant to my family:

_____

_____

_____

HOW to Do Research

We've been talking about WHY to do research and WHAT to research; now let's turn to some tips on HOW to do it.

First, before you start, think about how you are going to take notes and organize your findings. When I wrote my dissertation in the early 1990s, I took all my notes by hand on three-by-five-inch index cards, which I kept in little plastic boxes. Today you can set up folders on your computer where you can keep notes, save screenshots and photographs, and store links to things you read online. If you like to take lots of photographs of books and articles in the library and then read them later, you can invest time into learning new software, like Tropy, especially meant for organizing large research projects. Or—if you prefer to write on paper—you might get a special notebook; it will come in handy both for your background research and when you start to do your interviews. How you organize those index cards, notebooks, or digital folders will depend on how your own brain works and what will make it easiest for you to find what you need. It's a good idea to set up a system at the beginning of a project; just know that you can adjust as you move forward, depending on how the project evolves.

Background research for oral history projects can take several forms. Professional historians use two kinds of sources, which we call *secondary* and *primary sources.*

Secondary Sources

Secondary sources are published books and articles in which another historian or other expert, who has already done a lot of research, tells you about the subject you are interested in. So, for instance, if your family moved north during the Great Migration, when many Black families moved north to escape poverty and racism in the South, you might want to read Isabel Wilkerson's *The Warmth of Other Suns*, or Nicholas Lemann's *The Promised Land: The Great Black Migration and How It Changed America*. You could also watch documentaries or even listen to some podcasts that share reliable historical content.

One way to go about your research is to read a broad overview of American history in the twentieth century. Especially if it's been a while since you took a history class in high school or college, this will give you a sense of the broad sweep of change over time and how specific events like the Depression, the civil rights movement, Watergate, or the women's movement changed things. You can get a feel for the major policy shifts that happened during a particular president's time in office, which might provide you with some ideas for questions to ask your family members. What do they remember about President Carter's term in office and how his approach to governing

affected them? What was their opinion of Ronald Reagan and his reshaping of American policies? See the appendix for a list of overviews of American history in the twentieth and twenty-first centuries; you can read them from cover to cover, or seek out information on the eras and issues that are most germane to your family.

If you want, you could then do more focused research on a particular topic or geographic area that might be particularly relevant. Your local librarian can help you identify sources that will help provide context for your own family's history. Based on your initial reading, you could come to the library with a list of time periods or social issues about which you want to learn more. For example, perhaps your family felt strongly about unions, for or against—your librarian might help you find some readings about labor history or about a particular strike in the factory where your uncle worked, or near where you grew up. Maybe your mother was the first woman in her family to go to college and to have a career; your librarian can suggest some readings on women and higher education or on the women's movement that might give you some useful background information before you interview her. Reading secondary sources can help you understand the broader context for your own family's experiences and will give you ideas for questions to ask that you might not have thought of otherwise.

Selected Types of Secondary Sources Useful for History Research:

* Magazine or journal articles that present an argument about the past
* Textbooks
* Popular or scholarly books about the past
* Biographies
* Encyclopedias
* Dissertations and master's theses
* Wikipedia entries

Time periods I might be interested in:

_____

_____

_____

_____

_____

_____

What research questions do I have about the time period that a librarian could help me answer?

_____

_____

_____

_____

_____

_____

I *highly* recommend going to your public library and asking your reference librarian for help. In addition to your local public library, you may have access to a public university or college library near you; sometimes as a resident of the town or state, you can get access to a library card there, too. Reference librarians are some of the most helpful people on the planet, and believe it or not, they can help you find information that just will not come up on on Google or ChatGPT.

Of course, sometimes you're going to want to just look stuff up on Wikipedia, and that's okay. But it's important to remember that Wikipedia isn't "the whole truth and nothing but the truth." For instance, there are far more Wikipedia articles about men than about women, and many women who did really important things do not have their own Wikipedia page. To take just one example, as of this writing, Dianne Croteau, who invented the CPR mannequin on which so many people train to save lives, does not have an entry in Wikipedia. Wikipedia is an amazing tool, but if you really want to get a sense of how things changed over time and especially in your own family's backyard, I highly recommend asking a local librarian to help you find some other resources.

There are other online resources that you can get access to for free, as well. The Smithsonian, the Library of Congress, the National Archives, and PBS all have educational materials available on their websites. You can use Google Scholar to search for historical articles and books. Some links may be behind a paywall, but some will be available to read for free.

As of this writing, AI is developing rapidly but is not yet a completely trustworthy source for historical research. It is still too full of "hallucinations" and mistakes, and draws information from sources that are not always reliable. So while you can certainly ask it questions, it will be worth your time to check the sources it's drawing from and make sure that its answers are supported elsewhere.

List of secondary sources that my librarian recommended or that I found
online that I want to read:

_____

_____

_____

_____

_____

_____

Primary Sources

Whereas secondary sources are usually written after the events under consideration happened, primary sources are those that come from the time period itself. When I was studying the Civil War for my dissertation, I read the minutes of ladies' aid societies that were raising funds and assembling supplies in cities and towns across the Union for soldiers in the field; I read petitions from women to Abraham Lincoln, urging him to send home their sons who had run off to the army and lied about their ages; I read journals of girls and women living at home without their fathers and sons and brothers; I read letters between husbands in the army and their wives on the home front. I'll never forget crying in the archives after getting to the end of a box of letters between a loving couple to find the final one the wife received, starting with the dreaded "We regret to inform you . . ." These are all examples of primary sources—things that can help you understand directly how people at the time experienced the world around them.

The Civil War was over a hundred and fifty years ago, but primary sources are valuable even if the time they describe is more recent. Take my father: Another piece of the puzzle that helped him tell our family's story fell into place when my brother Ethan searched the online database of ship passengers through the Statue of Liberty–Ellis Island Foundation's website. Ethan found the manifest of the SS *Polonia*, which listed my grandparents by name and the day they arrived at Ellis Island. He gave my father an image of it and a photograph of the ship itself. This is a remarkable example of the riches that exist online—treasure troves of primary sources that libraries, archives, and organizations have made available for people to search and find, often free of charge.

In addition to those you can find online—the Ellis Island Foundation, the Library of Congress, the National Archives, and the Smithsonian, for instance, make millions of primary sources available to everyone—there are lots of others that you'll only find in person. If you want to find out what life in your hometown was like in the 1950s and '60s, you will want to go to your local library or historical society to see what they can show you. You might be amazed to find out what they have! You could find maps and photographs that show you how drastically things have changed—or how fundamentally the same they still are. You might find newspapers that can help you see how local people reacted to major events like the closing of a local hospital or a hurricane that wiped out a whole neighborhood, which could help you understand your own family's memories of the same event. There might be business directories that list every shop in town, where you could see your own family business as well as who the competition was. There might be records from local organizations— like the garden club your Aunt Mildred loved so much. You might discover they got their start by helping neighbors grow victory gardens during World War II. These are all examples of primary sources.

You can also do exciting detective work by looking at home. Here is where your family's own archive becomes important. You might be thinking, *Don't be ridiculous. We don't have a family archive.* But you probably have more than you realize. In fact, your home is likely *filled* with primary sources! Are there file cabinets in the basement with old school report cards, car loans, mortgages, and tax records? Shoeboxes in the attic filled with letters? Photo albums? Old diaries, maybe even with a tiny little lock and key? A box in the kitchen filled with old recipes? Below are some types of primary sources you might find in your own home.

* Photo albums
* Scrapbooks
* Baby books
* School yearbooks
* Correspondence: letters, postcards, birthday cards, invitations
* Diaries
* Memoirs
* Appointment books and calendars
* Report cards and other school files
* School projects
* Children's artworks
* Tax, bank, and credit card records
* House deeds
* Receipts
* Recipes, menus, shopping lists
* Club or volunteer organization minutes or records

If you have easy access to these sources, you could go through some of these materials in advance of your interviews, reading as much as possible. What's in those boxes up in the attic, and what can you learn about your family from them? Did your aunt cut out recipes from magazines and keep detailed menus for dinner parties? You could ask her about why she did that, and what some of her favorite recipes were, and who was at some of her most memorable dinner parties. Where did she learn to be such a good hostess? Why was throwing a nice party important to her? Maybe you discovered that your dad kept receipts for every purchase he ever made. What if you could look through those folders and start to get a sense of what he liked to spend money on and where he tried to save? You could then ask him about his attitudes toward earning, saving, and spending money. What lessons had he learned as a young boy about money, and from whom? What were some memorable purchases that he made, and what did they mean to him, looking back? What advice would he give his younger self about money?

Some primary sources might raise more questions than they answer. For instance, perhaps there are letters to your father from somebody whose name you don't recognize. Maybe there are photographs from a trip when your mother was young that you don't remember hearing about. As you look through the primary sources, you can start to jot down questions to ask during your interviews. You could show her the photo album and look through it together, with the recorder going, and she could talk to you about the people she sees, who they were, what they meant to her, what role they played in her life. Maybe you could ask your mom what she remembers about that particular trip, and then ask her about travel in general. How often did her family take vacations? What were some of the most memorable destinations they visited, and why did she enjoy them? Primary sources from your family's own collections are a great way to help you choose the direction of your project.

Please note, though, that if your family did not save a lot of primary sources—or if for instance they were lost during a flood, a fire, or during many moves from place to place—do not despair. While primary documents can be useful springboards, you can still do wonderful interviews without them. In fact, that makes your efforts to capture family members' memories even more important!

Some ideas of family primary sources I could look at and where they are:

_____

_____

_____

_____

_____

_____

Creating Timelines

Using secondary and primary sources can help you create a timeline of a person's life, which is often a useful first step in planning an interview. Having a set of basic dates can help you think about how their life fits into the chronology of your family story and into the narrative of your town or the country as a whole. Write down what you know about the person. Where and when were they born? Where did they grow up, go to school, get their first job? Put the dates in, in chronological order, and then, if you want, you could jot down notes in the margins about what was happening in your hometown or in the country around the same time that might have affected them (refer to the list of events on pages 46–49 if you do). Doing this will help you get your thoughts organized and help you see patterns. Maybe, for instance, there is a long gap between when Aunt Mildred graduated from college and when you met her as a child . . . What did she do during that time before you knew her? If you realize that was during the time of major demonstrations against the Vietnam War in the same city where she lived, you could ask her what she thought about those: Did she know people who went to war? How did that time period affect her and her feelings about politics, the military, the country?

 ## *Keeping Track of Sources, Both Primary and Secondary*

If you end up doing significant background research, you'll want to keep track of what you read, so that later you can find the information again and properly cite these other works. Citation is important, especially if you may want to donate your materials to an archive or share them with audiences outside your family. But even just for the purpose of helping family members understand where you got your background material from, it's a good idea to create a bibliography. If you mention an idea from a work in your final product, you can include the author and title of the book at the end or in the relevant paragraph. If you directly quote from these works in your final product, you should use footnotes or endnotes to give credit to the authors whose works you are citing. (For examples, you can watch for citations as you read this book and turn to the back to see my bibliography and suggested further readings.)

Why, you might be thinking, *do I need to keep track of information if I'm not in school anymore?* Mostly, I think of it as just the right thing to do. It's like letting somebody know that you got the recipe for that amazing cake you brought to the potluck from your Aunt Sally. Sure, you baked the cake, but you got the idea and many of the techniques from Sally, and she deserves some credit for that. Citing your sources is part of the process of doing responsible research. It's not about proving that you read a certain number of books or that you know how to jump through hoops. It's about giving credit where credit is due. If you are relying on the information that you found in someone else's book or article, and you quote from it or borrow ideas from it, you should let your readers know where and from whom you found it. That way, if somebody wants to go back to the article, book, or primary source you cited, whether they want to read it because you found it so interesting or because they think you might have made a mistake, providing footnotes, endnotes, and/or a bibliography makes that possible.

There are some great resources online, like Zotero, which is free and makes it much easier to keep track of your sources and compile bibliographies. You just enter the information into the website, and it will automatically format citations for you and create a full bibliography at the end. So much easier than when I was in school!

There are different styles of citations, and you can choose from among them. Libraries often have websites that will teach you how to properly cite sources. Most historians use what is called *The Chicago Manual of Style*. It has a website with a citation guide that clearly explains how to cite different types of sources. For instance, my father's memoir appears in my bibliography this way:

Seidman, Irving. *So You Might Know: A Memoir of My Parents.* Published by the author, Off the Common Books, 2014.

Your Research and Your Audience

Going back to your audience: Even if lots of details from in-depth background research intrigue you, if you plan on sharing your project with children, remember to think about how to hold the kids' attention. That's not to say research would be worthless; there are bound to be ways that you could use some of your research to help even the youngest audiences start to understand how your family's experience was similar or different from others'. For instance, if one of your family members talks about how theirs was the first family on the block to get a television, research could help youngsters understand when TVs were invented, when they became ubiquitous in family homes, and so on. You could even have the children look up that information! But with young children, in general, I think focusing on the stories will likely be most effective.

With young adult and adult audiences, you will have wider latitude for sharing more background research. Indeed, they might welcome having a sense of the broader historical context for your family's experiences. You could do background research on what was happening in the nation during the time period you're focusing on, or you could learn more about the specific place where your family members lived, what was happening there at that time, and how your family's story was similar to or different from others' in the same area.

Especially if your audience will include people who are external to your family, you are likely going to want to do more background research to put your family's story into the broader context of your local community or the nation's history. If you have a particular audience in mind (your town's social studies teachers, your congregation, or a local historical society, for instance), that can help you think about what information they might want to know. How many other churches, for instance, were there in the town when your cousin started hers? How many other female pastors were there? Can you look at the local business directory from the year your grandfather opened the hardware store to find out how many others there were, if any? Are there advertisements in the local newspaper showing what kinds of services and goods he offered? Maybe you can find newspaper articles about local women going to work in factories during World War II that help explain the wider impact of your great-grandmother's story.

A final note before you take off:

You've got this! Just like you'd load up the car with snacks and download your playlist if you were headed out on a road trip, you have now planned ahead for this project on which you're embarking. You've considered your motivations, your audiences, your scope, your resources, and your format. You've thought through doing background research, complete with citations. In the next part, we'll talk in detail about how to undertake the interviews themselves. Buckle up!

Part Two

The Interviews

N ot long ago, I decided spur of the moment to attend an estate sale in my Washington, DC, neighborhood. As I walked the few blocks to the address I'd seen advertised, I admired the beauty of the late-nineteenth-century row houses that line the streets where I live. I love their bay windows, turrets, and decorative brickwork. I didn't really need to buy anything; mostly, I wanted the chance to see inside one of these historic homes. As I ambled down the sidewalk, I hoped that the house hadn't been renovated too much—as a historian, I always regret it when the original moldings and fireplaces and other pieces of charming old architecture have been stripped away.

As soon as I climbed the front steps and went in through the door, I understood this estate sale had not been quickly thrown together by a bereaved family member—clearly, professionals had been called in, and for good reason. In the kitchen alone, there were hundreds of plates, cups, bowls, platters, glasses, pitchers, vases, and cutlery, impressively organized by type and boxed up in sets, with prices neatly marked on matching labels. I was stunned by the sheer volume of table settings, but the kitchen was just the beginning—in every corner of the old house, there were many neatly arranged piles of somebody's worldly possessions, obviously amassed over many decades, if not passed down for generations.

As I joined the two dozen other people who were peering at furniture and opening cupboards, I tried to imagine the individual through whose home I was traipsing. She must have liked to entertain, I thought.

I descended down creaky, narrow stairs into an unfinished basement that featured an impressive if somewhat quirky wine collection on open wooden shelves. From their labels, I sensed someone who liked to acquire a wide variety of bottles on their travels to faraway places. Back upstairs in the living room and hallways, art was stacked, leaning against the walls, and in a bedroom and home office, piles and piles of books spoke to a lifetime of collecting by someone with a wide-ranging and curious mind.

The staircase to the second floor had a chair lift, and into my head drifted an image of an elderly widow, slowly ascending to her bedroom after eating alone, her kitchen overflowing with porcelain and crystal reminders of dinner parties long ago. Suddenly, I was overcome with sadness. My afternoon walk down the block had given me an almost too intimate peek into the corners of an anonymous person's life, yet I had no real knowledge about who she was or how she lived or what her laugh sounded like. A life's worth of possessions that once meant something well beyond their monetary value were now displayed to strangers' eyes, ready to be sold off, detached from their context. Each piece of furniture, each knickknack had a story, but I couldn't hear what it had to say. It was all too much for me, and I left in a hurry.

As I walked home, I thought about how much better it would have felt if the objects had not just price tags but story labels attached to them. I should say that, in addition to my work as an oral historian, I am also a curator at a history museum, and so I've had some practice writing labels about objects. That day, I made up a character in my mind and imagined the possibilities. She liked to entertain, to travel, to learn. At one point, she needed help to get up the stairs. "This is the cake stand Mrs. Navarro inherited from her grandmother, which she brought out for special family occasions. She was especially known for her chocolate coconut cake." "Whenever one of her grandchildren turned ten years old, they got to drink sparkling apple cider from one of these crystal glasses for the first time." "Mrs. Navarro's best childhood chum brought this small painting back from a trip she took to Vietnam and gave it to her as a testament to their long friendship." "A secret admirer sent Mrs. Navarro this bracelet on Valentines Day in 1969, but she never found out who the person was." I created Mrs. Navarro out of thin air, but it got me thinking about how connected our stories often are to objects.

I started to imagine what I might have learned had I had the opportunity to interview my former neighbor. Even though I'd never met her—in fact, I don't really know for sure whether the former owner of that house was a woman or a man—I was curious. My Capitol Hill neighborhood has its own long-running oral history project, where local volunteers interview other people who live "on the Hill." They share the interviews online, and before I moved here, I had spent hours reading and learning about my new neighborhood, past and present. If I could have interviewed Mrs. Navarro, I might have sat with her in her sunny kitchen at the back of her house and asked her about when and how she had come to live in it. I could have asked her to tell me about the pretty china that she was serving tea and cookies on—did she purchase it, or had she inherited it? Did it have special meaning to her, and if so, why? Did she entertain often? For fun or for work? What were some of her most memorable dinner parties? Who taught her to cook, to set a table, how to arrange flowers in those colorful vases she displayed on her shelves? I might have asked her to tell me about the trips on which she collected artwork, or to talk to me about the wine bottles in the basement. I would love to have asked her about the piles of books that were overflowing her bookshelves—what had her formal education been like, and how did she decide what to read next? Did she participate in book clubs, or did she prefer to read on her own? Was she influenced by things like bestseller lists, or booksellers' recommendations, or did she have an internally guided approach to what appeared to be a voracious reading habit? What did she think about the rise of social media—did she participate at all? Why or why not? What did she think about the state of the world today, and how did it compare with her memories of growing up, coming of age, and her many years of living in Washington, DC? By starting with questions about the material objects with which she surrounded herself, I could explore avenues into her personal history—her family, her work, her travels, her attitudes and values, and her insights into the world around us.

Our homes are filled with objects that can help us learn about the past—whether dishes in the china cabinet, bicycles and toys in the garage, tools in the basement workshop, record albums in the den, linens in the closet, Christmas decorations in the attic . . . you get the idea. Many of these objects hold stories; they are imbued with meaning because of who gave them to us, or how we felt when we used them, or with whom we've shared them over time. Museum people call these objects *material culture*.

It was too late for me to ask my neighbor about all the amazing things she had collected. The experience in that house made me think about the one in which I grew up, and my mother, who, now in her eighties, has been enthusiastically engaged in the process of "Swedish death cleaning" over

 the last few years. In this practice, described by Margareta Magnusson in her book *The Gentle Art of Swedish Death Cleaning: How to Free Yourself and Your Family from a Lifetime of Clutter*, the goal is to clear out things that are not important to you before you die, to lessen the burden on your surviving family. I'm grateful to my mom for taking on this task—as an archivist herself, she has long had the instinct to hold on to things, and the house she and my dad have lived in for over fifty years has many closets and basement shelves and cupboards full of stuff. It truly is a gift to my brother and me for her to begin the sorting process.

What I started to think about, though, is not what she let go of, but what was left. How everything that remains must be important to my mother—there must be a story to it, a reason she kept it. My goal now is to learn more about the decisions she made and to have her pass on to us as many of those stories as possible before it is too late. I'm eager to hear her tell me about the linens her mother, grandmother, and aunts sewed and embroidered. At our wedding, my husband and I stood under a chuppah—a wedding canopy signifying the new home a Jewish couple will create together—that my mom crafted from a lace tablecloth her grandmother had sewn. My brother and then, decades later, my daughter were married under the same chuppah. Sometimes objects collect more and more layers of meaning as they get passed down through generations. Learning what we can about those layers of meaning is a window into learning about our loved ones and the stories they hold dear.

What would I have asked Mrs. Navarro, and what will I ask my mom when the time comes? What might you ask your family members when you sit down with them?

As we covered in the previous part, there are many motivations for undertaking oral histories with your family, and the resulting interviews can take different forms to meet your goals. I use my neighbor's house and my mom's remaining possessions as examples of how objects might fuel your curiosity and guide your investigations. But you might be inspired by wanting to know more about a particular event in your family's past, or even why certain traditions have been handed down. No matter why you want to do your interviews or about what, there are certain fundamental aspects to interviewing someone that remain the same.

In this part, we'll review some of the most important dos and don'ts of interviewing that apply in most cases. We'll go over some basic information to consider about where and when to do your interviews, what kinds of equipment you might use, and some tips for recording. I'll review potential topics for you to focus on and provide sample questions you can ask. I'll also share some guidance on how to structure your own questions, based on your interests and particular situation. I have some suggestions for how to ask good follow-up questions, too—and some ideas on overcoming challenges that might arise. We'll talk about how to reflect on your interviews and learn from your experience so that you can feel more and more comfortable as you develop your skills over time.

Finally, we'll also cover other ways of gathering family stories beyond interviews—perhaps less traditional approaches, but ones that will nevertheless deepen your sense of connection to family members, provide you with more understanding of your family's past, and create lasting bonds and traditions you can carry with you into the future.

When I taught oral history methods, I used to tell my students that the most important tools they needed to bring with them to the interview were their curiosity, their respect for their interviewee, and their commitment to listening deeply. If you show up with all of these, I assured them, no matter what happens, your interview will be a success. I stand by that advice.

An oral history interview can be a memorable, even profound experience for both the interviewer and the interviewee. I had a student once, a member of the football team at the university where I was working, who told me that after completing his first-ever oral history interview with a local woman in her seventies, he thought about everyone he passed on the street differently—especially the "old ladies." He now realized that everyone carries a story within them and that their stories are far more fascinating than he had previously imagined. His whole view of his community had changed.

For those interviewed, too, the experience can be powerful. I once interviewed a woman in Minnesota who had come to this country as a refugee from Laos; her family belongs to the Hmong ethnic group. She told me that Hmong women rarely got to participate in the centrally important storytelling traditions of their culture. As a result, she found the opportunity to share her life history over several hours to be deeply meaningful on a personal level. And because it was so powerful for her, it prompted her to think about how to incorporate more chances for other people to share their stories into her professional life as well.

I encourage you to try undertaking at least one oral history interview, because I believe so strongly in the power of that approach. If you are worried about not being an expert, don't be! You will grow as an interviewer—it is a skill that you can hone and improve. You don't need to be perfect; there is no such thing as a perfect interview. Even professional oral historians make plenty of mistakes, and we all learn by doing. With this book as a foundation, you're off to a great start.

I'll talk about oral history methods in the pages that follow. You may decide that, in the context of your family history project, different methods could complement your purposes, or perhaps even better serve them. In that case, go for it! Toward the end of part 2, you'll find some suggestions for other ways to gather and share your family history. But below are my top tips for approaching an oral history interview; I hope they help you feel confident that you can take on this compelling form of research.

 ## *Setting Yourself Up for Success*

The most important first step to becoming a great interviewer is to tap into an honest curiosity about the other person's life. Even if you think you've heard your grandfather's stories a million times, when you decide to interview him, do so with the mindset that there is more for you to learn about him—and from him. Stay open to the opportunities that the interview will present you with the opportunity to go beyond the handful of stories you've heard before. I have seen students show up to an interview with a list of questions that they rush through so quickly the person being interviewed barely has a chance to talk. For the best results, you need to show up with your whole self and make room for the other person's whole self as well. The goal is not to check off some boxes on a list of questions or to simply gather a set of facts. It is to give the other person a chance to share their story, their experiences, their perspective on the past and their reflections on the world around them—and for you to embrace the privilege of receiving that gift. Let's get you ready for that experience.

As a relative, you already have an advantage over an outsider coming in to do an oral history interview: Presumably, your interviewee already trusts you to a significant degree. You most likely hold a shared set of connections and perhaps even values and worldview. So, unlike if I or one of my former students showed up to interview your family member, you probably do not need to prove your trustworthiness or establish rapport. Nevertheless, you still want to make your interviewee feel at ease and to show that you are taking the interview seriously. You want to convey that you care about them and their story.

A Promise I'm Making to Myself:

I, ————————————————— (name), will try to stay open to the opportunities that my interviews will present—even if I've heard some of the stories before!

————————————————
(signature)

Show Them You Care

So how will the other person know that you care and are showing up with an honest, open curiosity? There are a few key signs you can give them in the way you approach the interview. Some of these steps might seem obvious, but they are important nevertheless.

❋ **Eliminate distractions so that you can focus completely on the person you are interviewing.**

• **Create a special appointment for the interview**—set aside some time in both of your schedules when you won't need to worry about picking up somebody from school, or answering work calls, or juggling other responsibilities.

Block out a few hours where this interview can be your singular focus.

• **Choose a place for the interview where you will both be comfortable and where ideally you won't be interrupted.** If you are recording the interview, be sure you are in a quiet place—you don't want a lot of background noise like at a coffee shop or restaurant, because you risk not being able to hear their voice clearly. A little ambient noise is okay—one of my very favorite recordings of an interview was done by a graduate student sitting with her interviewee on a porch swing in rural Appalachia; you can hear the birds chirping and the sounds of children playing in the distance. As the woman talks about her life, you get an audible sense of her surroundings, even though you can't see them.

• **You may use your cell phone as a recording device (as we'll discuss later in this part), but that is the only role your phone should play during the interview.** Turn it to airplane mode so that you don't receive calls, texts, or alerts that might distract you and interrupt the flow of your conversation.

✳ Use body language to communicate interest and engagement.

• **Sit up, facing your interviewee.** Don't slouch or sit in a way that might convey boredom.

- **Make eye contact and smile.** You might be listening to your interviewee for a long time—potentially for more than an hour or two. They will gather energy from you if you use your face to suggest continued interest and engagement; if they sense you are getting bored or distracted, they are likely to start shutting down or rushing through their story.

- **In a formal oral history interview, you try not to use your own voice much except to ask your questions**—the idea is for the focus to stay on the interviewee—so you try not to say things like "Uh-huh," "Of course," "Yes, exactly," or all the other things we usually do to express agreement. It's hard! But you can use your eyes and smile, nod, and the like, so that they know you are listening closely. On the other hand, you may not be interested in the niceties of a formal oral history interview and want instead to have more of a recorded conversation between the two of you; if so, then you are free to respond, offer your own opinions, memories, and so on. Remember, this is not an assignment—there is no one right way to do this. Decide what is most important to you, and follow your instincts as to what method will work best and get you the kind of results you want.

How I'll Get Started:

When might be a good time for my first interview?

_____

_____

_____

_____

_____

Where might I conduct my interview?

_____

_____

_____

_____

_____

 Deep Listening

No matter what, pay close attention. In general, most of us can usually sense when somebody is really paying attention to us and when they are just faking it. So don't fake it. It's hard work to pay close attention for extended periods—if you find yourself getting distracted, just bring your attention back to the person's story. Paying really close attention means listening on several different levels, and watching, too:

* **What are they saying?** Be sure you are tracking the story they are telling you. If you are recording the interview, you don't need to take copious notes—it's better to continue making eye contact than to be focused on a notebook or computer screen. But it is a good idea to have a pen and paper with you; you might jot down a few key moments here and there. I often note when there is something I want to come back to with a follow-up question. That way, I don't have to interrupt them while they are in the flow of telling a story, but I won't forget the questions it raised in my mind, and I can return to it when there is a pause.

* **Are there hidden messages in the words they are using?** For instance, most parents know that if a teenager answers a question by mumbling, "I don't know," it usually means "I don't want to talk about it." My father, who wrote his own book about interviewing as a research methodology,[*] taught me to notice how when somebody talks about a "challenge" they had "overcome," they often are skipping over the hard parts and not sharing the true nature of the experience they had endured. We've been taught to package our stories in palatable ways for college applications, job applications, watercooler conversations, and dinner parties. If you think your interviewee is sidestepping difficult aspects of their story, you might offer them an opportunity to share more fully with you, a trusted listener. "That must have been really hard, Uncle Joe, when you lost your job. I know you got a new one six months later, but what were you most worried about before that came through?"

✳ **What are they *not* saying?** Do there seem to be gaps or silences, things they avoid talking about? Many, many people will say in interviews that "we didn't know we were poor." They'll focus on the happier memories, the family warmth or community cohesion. Those, of course, are vitally important pieces of the story. But can you find ways to get behind the nostalgia a little bit, to understand the harder realities of their lives? You might ask them something like, "Looking back, what do you realize now about your family's economic situation that maybe you didn't understand at the time?"

---

* Irv Seidman, *Interviewing as Qualitative Research: A Guide for Researchers in Education and the Social Sciences*, 5th ed. (Teachers College Press, 2019).

✳ **What can you glean from nonverbal cues?** I once listened to the recording of an interview a graduate student had done with a woman in her fifties, an entrepreneur in the South. Every time the woman mentioned her father, she laughed. What the student hadn't noticed, though, was that the laughter was clearly a kind of nervous tic, a cover-up for some sort of uncomfortable emotion. When I mentioned my hunch to her, my student realized that by not paying enough attention to that uncomfortable laughter, she had missed an opportunity to ask some important follow-up questions that could have helped her understand more fully the woman's relationship with her father and how it had shaped her career.

✳ **What is their body language telling you?** Do they seem relaxed, or are their arms crossed over their chest, or shoulders raised high up near their ears? Maybe they are turned away from you or in other ways signaling that they might be feeling uncomfortable? If so, you need to use your best instincts to think through how to respond. Are they just getting used to the interview process and will loosen up over time? Or are you asking questions that make them anxious? You might be able to figure it out on your own, or you could also ask them directly: "I notice you look a little ill at ease at the moment. Is there something we could do to help you feel more relaxed?" If you bring a notebook—and I think that's a good idea; more on tools shortly—you can also jot down that they seemed uncomfortable when certain topics come up, or whatever you think is causing the problem. You might find that when you go back and listen to the interview, it becomes clear what the problem was. It's a good way to learn to be aware of what's happening in the moment, even if you never figure out exactly why they seemed tense.

✱ By setting a welcoming tone for the interview and by paying careful attention to the conversation, you will convey your respect for your interviewee and a keen interest in their story. That is the most important way to set yourself up for success.

How I'll Prepare to Listen Deeply:

What's one action I want to focus on to convey I'm paying close attention?

_____

_____

_____

_____

_____

 *Creating the Interview Guide*

Of course, the results of your interviews will also be determined to a large degree by the questions you ask. Planning out some of those questions in advance is an important part of your preparation. In general, I suggest going into an interview with a prepared set of questions, but also being ready to be flexible and responsive to your interviewee as the process unfolds.

Usually, I will prepare an interview guide—a list of questions that I have written out based on my background research and the kinds of information I'm hoping to hear (refer to part 1!). I will circle or highlight the ones that I want to be absolutely sure I get answered before the interview is over. The rest are there to serve as a kind of outline for the interview, and although I hope to get to most of them, I'm aware that the story may unfold differently from how I imagined.

In this way, an oral history interview is very different from a survey. You may have taken a political survey over the phone or online at some point, or even been approached by someone at a store looking for feedback on the customer experience. In a survey, an interviewer will ask everyone the same questions; they have a script, and they will follow that script closely. Oral history interviews are different. We say they are "co-created" between the interviewer and the interviewee: You will guide the interview with your questions but also, to some degree, follow the lead of your interviewee so that you can be sure to capture the story they want to share. While you might be interested in particular topics, you also want to be sure that they have the chance to communicate what is most important to them.

The resulting interview will be shaped by the relationship between the people involved. If I were to interview your grandmother, even if I asked her the same questions you did, she might answer differently. For example, there might be some stories she would not want to discuss with me but would be happy for you to know, and there also might be some topics she'd be more comfortable discussing with a stranger than with those who know and love her best. No one interview will be "right," perfect, or the whole truth. But each one will capture a person's stories, memories, and reflections in that shared moment with the interviewer—and that is what matters most.

Life Histories and Topical Interviews

Oral historians talk about two broad types of interviews— *life history* and *topical* interviews. In life history interviews, the goal is to hear the individual narrate their own life experiences from childhood until today; the idea is to capture as much as possible about their whole lifespan. Topical interviews focus, you guessed it, on a particular topic. How you approach your family history will, again, depend on your own motivation, as discussed in part 1. So, for instance, you might decide you want to do life history interviews of your grandparents. On the other hand, you might want to do topical interviews with members of different generations focused on their memories of your family's summer beach vacations. Or you might want to interview your three aunts to learn more about the impact of Hurricane Katrina on your family's trajectory. In those cases, you might not spend as much time interviewing each person about their full lifespan but focus more closely on the particular subject you are most interested in.

Many interviews, of course, are a combination of life history and topical. Even when I am doing a set of interviews that are focused on a particular subject matter, I still ask people about their grandparents and their parents, their growing up, and so on, because it helps me understand why

they respond to certain events or issues in the ways that they do. For instance, if I'm interviewing a group of women and my topical focus is on their experiences with the women's rights movement in the 1970s, I won't dive right into that. I want to know what shaped their attitudes and where they were coming from: What kinds of messages did they receive about boys' and girls' roles as children? I might want to ask them about whether they had the same chores or different ones from their brothers and how they felt about that. Did their parents and grandparents encourage them to go to college? Did their grandmothers and mothers work outside the home? Which women influenced them the most as role models when they were growing up? Then when we get to the 1970s, I'll have a better understanding of why they responded as they did to feminist ideas.

As we saw earlier with the imaginary Mrs. Navarro, objects offer us a way into people's life stories. An interview that is focused on material culture—a collection of dolls or salt and pepper shakers, a bureau top full of costume jewelry, an attic full of quilts—is one kind of topical interview. You can consider whether you want to start with the objects, asking about each one in turn, or begin with some more traditional life history questions and then ask about the objects. Your choice might depend on the interviewee as well as on your own curiosity.

Whatever broad type of interview you choose to conduct, by preparing thoughtfully ahead of time, you'll set yourself up for success when you sit down to talk to your family member.

How I'll Approach My Interview:

Do I want to do life history interviews or topical interviews?

_____

_____

_____

_____

_____

_____

If topical, what will the focus be?

_____

_____

_____

_____

_____

Will material culture objects be important to my interview?
Why or why not?

_____

_____

_____

_____

_____

_____

If I want to focus on objects, which ones?

_____

_____

_____

_____

_____

_____

What Makes a Good Interview Question?

No matter which way you want to focus your interviews, there are certain characteristics that make for a good set of questions.

* **One at a time:** It may be tempting to ask a series of questions all at once, but try to ask just one at a time. For instance, rather than saying, "Tell me about your grandparents, and your parents, and your growing up," start with just one question. For instance, "What do you recall about the role your grandparents played in your childhood?"

* **Open-ended:** Avoid questions that can be answered by *yes* or *no* or other one-word responses. Instead, ask questions that encourage your interviewee to describe their memories more fully. So rather than "How many siblings do you have?" (to which you might just get a perfunctory, "Three"), you could say, "How would you describe your siblings?" Then you're likely to get the number, their names, their ages, and their most annoying or endearing characteristics.

* **Narrative, lyrical, and reflective:** I think of questions as coming in these three flavors. Using these different types of questions can help you get a multilayered, rich set of stories from your interviewee.

- **Narrative questions** are the most straightforward, where you are asking somebody to narrate something that happened in the past. "What happened when Uncle Joe lost his finger in the factory?" "What did you do on your first day on the job?" "How did you get from California to Minnesota?"

- **Lyrical questions** are those that try to get at the more emotional or descriptive elements of a story—imagine the kinds of details you might include if you were writing a poem about the same events. Ask questions that help you get at those details. "How did you feel when you learned that you would have to move out of your house?" "How would you describe the apartment you moved into next?" "What did your mother's perfume smell like?" It's amazing how asking about the weather on a particular day can sometimes trigger a flood of memories. Do you remember the weather on 9/11?

- **Reflective questions** give people a chance to reflect on their experiences from the perspective of the present. It's one of my favorite things about oral history—the ability to capture how somebody makes sense of the past today. Something that seemed terribly important when they were a teenager might not, from the vantage point of advanced age, loom as large in their life anymore. Or an event that seemed relatively mundane when it happened might have turned out to be transformative in the long run. Giving people a chance to reflect on the decisions they made and the changes they've seen over time is one of the best features of oral histories. "From where you sit today, Aunt Carol, how do you reflect on your decision to turn down that first marriage proposal to pursue your dream of becoming a journalist?" "Grandpa, knowing what you do now, what advice would you give your younger self about work and family?"

I think great interviews are often a combination of all three of these types of questions. You can decide how you want to mix and match them, and it might differ based on the communication style of your interviewee. If your interviewee is a good storyteller, you might never need to worry about any of this, because they naturally include the more lyrical and reflective responses to almost any question. But if your interviewee tends to stick closely to a "this happened and then that happened" type of recounting, you might try asking a few questions that prod them to share more about their emotions or their sensory experiences.

One more piece of advice before you begin writing your interview guide:

Arrange your questions in a logical order. Think of them as a sort of outline for the story you are hoping to get. You don't necessarily have to go in chronological order (you could, for instance, start by asking somebody to describe their current life and career, and then go back in time to trace their personal and professional development). But especially if you are undertaking a life history interview, it usually makes sense to take a straightforward approach. I often say that we can't really understand why a person approaches an issue or reacts to a situation in a particular way if we don't understand where they are coming from and how they arrived at that moment. Having your interviewee tell you first about their grandparents, their parents, and their childhood experiences can often help you get a base of understanding for why they made the decisions they did about their education, family life, career, and so on.

 *Building Your Interview Guide*

The following is a list of potential topics you could consider and some sample questions you could use. When you are ready, you can start to write up your own interview guide by compiling a set of questions that you are going to ask, using these as a starting point if you wish. Remember that this isn't a survey; while you can ask some of the same questions of different people, your interview guides should be tailored to each individual. Your background research may be helpful as you think about how to structure the interview. You can use these sample questions, rephrasing them to fit your own speaking style better; you can use a few from this list and then add more of your own; or you can ignore these completely and come up with your own unique approach.

In this list, I have started with life history questions that would likely apply to almost anyone, organized by life stage. I've included questions with a mix of narrative, lyrical, and reflective prompts. As you build your interview guide, try to include some of each kind. When you get the hang of open-ended questions of these different types, you will be able to craft your own.

The second part of the list offers some ideas for other themes that you could add into a life history interview or that might be the focus for a set of topical interviews. Remember the list of turning-point moments in American history from part 1? Consider which of those might be most relevant to your interviewee's life and add in questions about those as well. You can use these to practice building a set of your own open-ended questions.

Life History Questions

Family of Origin

* How well did you know your grandparents, and what role did they play in your life?

* When you were growing up, what stories did you hear about your ancestors?

* What do you know about how and when your family came to America?

* How would you describe the family you grew up in?

* What did your parents do to earn a living?

* From what you could tell, how did they feel about their work when you were young?

* How would you describe your parents' parenting style?

* How would you describe yourself as a child?

* What was your relationship like to your siblings?

* Were there similar or very different expectations for boys and girls, men and women in your family?

* Did you receive an allowance as a child, and if so, what did you spend it on?

* What do you recall about your family's experiences with money and/or debt?

* How would you describe the role of food, cooking, and meals in your family life?

* What role, if any, did organized religion play in your family's life?

* Looking back at your childhood, what were some of the most important messages that your family passed on to you, whether directly or indirectly, and how do you think they shaped you?

Home and Neighborhood

* How would you describe the neighborhood you lived in to someone who'd never been there?
* If I went over to your house or apartment, what might I have noticed walking in the front door?
* What do you remember about your childhood bedroom?
* What are some of your strongest sensory memories of your childhood home—are there smells, sounds, textures, or images that you associate with where you grew up?
* What was your town or city like when you were growing up, and how has it changed?

School and Friendships

* How did you feel about school as a child?
* Were there any teachers or school staff who were particularly important to you? Why or why not?
* How would you describe your childhood friendships?
* How did you spend your free time as a child?

* Were there any toys, games, or sports you remember particularly enjoying?

* How did you see yourself in relation to your neighbors and your peers at school?

Adolescence

* What do you remember about your experiences with puberty?

* How would your classmates and friends have described you in middle school and high school?

* What was your attitude toward school at that age and why?

* Were there any teachers or other school staff who were particularly important to your development at this stage?

* What hobbies or skills did you develop during adolescence?

* Did you work to earn money at this age, and if so, what did you do?

* Do you remember what you did with your first paycheck and how you felt about it?

* How did you and your friends spend your free time?

* How would you describe dating culture at that time?

* What, if any, experience did you have with dating as an adolescent?

* Were there any celebrities, books, movies, or albums that had a strong impact on how you saw the world at that age?

* What expectations did you have at that age for how your life would turn out?

* Looking back, how do you reflect on who you were at that stage of your life?

* What messages, if any, would you want to give your adolescent self if you could?

Higher Education

* What was your family's attitude toward higher education?

* What shaped your decision about whether or not to go to college?

* How big a role did money play in your decisions about higher education?

* What were your expectations about what college would be like?

* How did your experience match or differ from your expectations?

* Who were some of the most important friends you made in college?

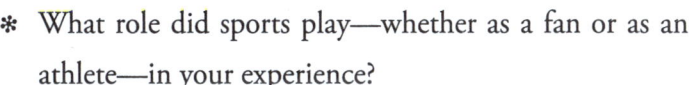

* What courses, teachers, or advisors had the biggest impact on you?
* How did you pick a major, and what did you like most about it?
* How would you describe your social life in college?
* What role did sports play—whether as a fan or as an athlete—in your experience?
* What was dating culture like at that time, and to what degree did you participate?
* How significant was your college experience and the choices you made there in shaping you as an adult?

Work/Career

* What messages did you receive from your family growing up about work, money, and careers?
* What messages did you absorb from popular culture, school, or your friends about work, money, and careers?
* How did you choose a career or job path for yourself?
* How would you describe your early work experiences?
* What are some of your favorite memories from some of your early work experiences?
* What were some of the hardest aspects of starting out working as a young adult?

* What role, if any, did mentors play in your career?

* What kinds of relationships did you have with your colleagues and fellow workers?

* How did your career or job path develop over time?

* How would you describe a typical day at work for you?

* What were some important turning points in your work life over time?

* Was work a big source of your identity or not so much?

* What are you most proud of in terms of your work or career?

Partners/Marriage/Family

* When you were growing up, what were your expectations for yourself in terms of relationships, marriage, and family?

* How closely did your experiences match or differ from what you expected?

* If married:
  • How did you meet your spouse?
  • Describe for me one of your early dates—where did you go, what did you see, do, eat?
  • How/when did you decide to get married?
  • What was your wedding like?

- What do you think are the most important aspects to a strong marriage?
- What are the skills you need to develop to stay married?

* If single, widowed, or divorced:
    - How did you come to be single as an adult?
    - What do you like most about being single?
    - What has been the hardest part?
    - How did your parents react to your decision to stay single?
    - How do you think our culture does or does not support single people?
    - What would you like to share about your divorce and its impact on you?
    - I'm sure that losing your spouse must have had a tremendous impact on you. What can you share about that time and how that loss has shaped your experience?

- How did you experience grief, and what lessons learned would you want to share with others?
- Where do you find your most important sources of emotional support and companionship?

✽ If a parent:
- What do you remember most about when your children were born?
- What are some of your beliefs about parenting?
- What are some of your favorite memories about your early days of parenting?
- What are some of the hardest parts about parenting?
- How have you and your spouse managed caring for your children?
- How did having children affect your career, if at all, and your ideas about work and family?
- What are some of the most important messages you have tried to pass on to your children?

✽ If not a parent:
- What factors led to you not having children?
- What have been the positive parts about that?

- Have there been hard parts about it, and if so, what are they?
- How have people responded to you not having children?

* How would you describe the role of our extended family in your own life?
* What kinds of family stories or lore have been passed down?
* How do those stories shape your own attitudes toward life?
* Can you describe the role of "chosen family" members— people who are not related by blood or law but who you consider part of your family?
* What non–family member had the greatest impact on you or your family, and how would you describe that impact?

Health, Illness, Aging, Death, and Dying

* What have been some ways that changing health or illness has shaped your life experience?
* Can you tell me about any experiences with receiving medical care that felt important to you?
* How would you say the medical system has changed over your lifetime?
* How would you describe your own role in providing

care for family members who are/were dealing with a health issue?

- * Are there family recipes, beliefs, or practices for maintaining health or treating illness that have been passed down?

- * (If a woman): How did you experience menopause, and how has it shaped your outlook, if at all?

* How has growing older affected your outlook on life?

* What new skills, talents, or personality traits have you developed later in life?

* Have there been family experiences with death or dying that have had a major impact on you, and if so, how would you describe the impact of those losses?

* How has your family dealt with grief?

* Are there any important family traditions surrounding dying, death, burial, or grieving that have been passed down through the generations?

Historical Change over Time

* What have been some of the most important cultural changes you've observed over time, whether at the personal, local, or national level?

* What do you think is the most important historical moment you lived through?
* Looking back, how did that event/moment affect your own life directly or indirectly?

Write your interview guide. Star the five most important questions.

Ten questions from the list above I want to use:

Some questions of my own, including narrative, lyrical, and reflective:

_____

_____

_____

_____

_____

_____

_____

_____

_____

_____

Topical Questions:

Using the list of turning point moments in American history from part 1, your knowledge of your family, and your background research, you could develop a set of questions on specific historical moments and themes that are of particular interest to you and relevant to your family.

* Choose a legal turning point that had an impact on your family, whether positive or negative: GI Bill, integration, immigration laws, Title IX, marriage equality, and so on.

* Explore the impact of a particular war or military engagement on your family member, whether they were in the armed forces or on the home front.

* Learn about their experience of one or more major historical moments—9/11, the COVID pandemic, or others—how they met those moments, and how they think those moments shaped their life afterward.

* Investigate their experience of an environmental or natural disaster (a flood, hurricane, chemical spill) that might have affected them.

* Ask about their experience with a social movement—civil rights, labor activism, peace movements, women's rights, the counterculture—to learn more about their involvement in or resistance to those movements and organizations.

* Connect your family history to news of the day. You could ask, for instance, about how their own experience with immigration or the stories passed down about their family's arrival in the United States shapes their attitudes toward debates around immigration today.

* Ask about the family's history of economics and class status. How do they understand their class status, and what markers do they use to understand that? Did it change over time?

* What role have popular culture and the media—movies, books, TV, newspapers, magazines, sports, video games, social media—played in your family over time and how has it changed?

Pick one of these topics and practice writing three open-ended questions about it; one each of narrative, lyrical, and reflective:

My topic is:

_____

_____

_____

1. _____

_____

2. _____

_____

_____

3. _____

_____

If you are focusing on material culture, you might consider the following questions as you write your interview guide:

* What can you tell me about this (object)?
* When did you acquire it?
* Why did you acquire it?
* What do you use it for?
* Do you know who made it?
* What can you tell me about that person?
* What is it made of?
* If someone gave it to you, what can you tell me about them?
* Why did they give it to you?
* How do you feel about this object?
* How do you feel when you use it?
* What do you think of when you look at it?
* Why is it important to you?
* What story do you think it tells about you or our family?

Are there material objects in my family in which I am interested? If so, which ones?

_____

_____

_____

_____

_____

Why do I think those might be interesting to learn about?

_____

_____

_____

_____

_____

What would I most want to know?

_____

_____

_____

_____

_____

_____

 **Skipping Questions**

Remember that your interview guide is just a guide; it's not a script. You *do not* have to ask every question on your list. By thinking ahead of time about what is most important to you to learn about, listening carefully to the answers provided, and following the thread of the stories that emerge, you may find that you go in new directions and don't get to every question you wrote down. That is perfectly okay and means you are doing oral history right!

Follow-Up Questions

Remember that the questions you write on your interview guide are only the beginning. Some of the most important questions you ask will be follow-up questions. You can't predict those in advance—they will arise from you listening deeply in the moment. On the other hand, there are some follow-up questions that work in many different situations, like: "How did that feel?" "Help me imagine the scene—can you tell me more about what you saw (or heard or smelled or felt) at that moment?" "Looking back on that time, how do you think about it now?"

I often use follow-up questions as a way to get an interviewee to give me more details that will help me see an event more clearly (lyrical follow-up questions) or understand the impact of an event on them (reflective follow-up questions). They can also be ways to simply encourage a reluctant narrator to keep talking, by showing you are truly interested in hearing more.

For instance, imagine a conversation that starts with a question you have written down:

You: Aunt Harriet, can you tell me about what it was like when Hurricane Floyd hit?

Aunt Harriet: Oh, it was terrible, just terrible. So awful. Hard to describe.

Here you might want to ask a follow-up question, rather than leaving the topic of this massive event without much understanding for how or why it was so terrible. Sometimes follow-up questions that focus on the senses can help interviewees tap into a more specific memory.

> **You:** Can you remember any particular sounds you heard during the storm?

> **Aunt Helen:** Oh yes. I remember we were hiding in the basement, and I could hear what sounded like a train rushing across the house above us. It was the wind itself, but I really thought that a train was hitting my home. That was one of the most upsetting things to me as a child.

Reflective prompts make good follow-up questions, asking the person to reflect on the event from their vantage point today.

> **You:** Wow, Aunt Harriet, that sounds awful. When you look back, what kind of impact do you think the hurricane had on your life?

> **Aunt Harriet:** Well, for one thing, I became much more scared of weather—darkening clouds and the wind picking up has made me anxious ever since. We lost friends who moved away after the storm, and that made me sad. I think I lost some sort of trust in the way things

are—I'm always aware of how quickly things can change. And of course, we lost family treasures, like our photo albums and all my mother's handmade dresses that we had stored in attic. I'm still here, we're still here, and I'm very grateful for that. But it really did upend a lot about our lives, and that's just a fact.

Learning when and how to ask follow-up questions takes practice. You can write out a few all-purpose ones at the top of your interview guide to remind yourself of potential ways to prod a little bit:

* Can you tell me more about that?
* What do you remember about how that looked/smelled/sounded/felt?
* How did you feel about that?
* Looking back, how do you think about that now?

My Go-To Follow-Up Questions:

Add a couple of all-purpose follow-up questions of your own here:

_____

_____

But there will be other follow-up questions that you just have to come up with on the spot, based on your own curiosity and your deep listening. And don't worry—no matter how well an interview goes, every interviewer recognizes that they missed some opportunities for asking a good follow-up question. I can't tell you how often, driving away from an interview, I get the urge to hit my forehead with my palm, suddenly realizing something I should have asked. It's hard, but you'll get better at it over time!

One thing you can do to improve is listen to other interviews and pay attention to how the interviewer handled follow-up questions. Did they do a good job? What would you have asked in that situation? You can listen to interviewers of different sorts—whether on NPR, *The Today Show*, or your favorite podcast. Pay attention to the questions they are asking—are they open-ended? Do they elicit colorful responses? Does the interviewer listen carefully and ask good follow-up questions? If you want to listen to oral historians specifically, in this book's appendix, there is a short list of oral history collections around the country that have some of their interviews available online—these are great resources!

After you've done an interview or two of your own, it's always a good idea to review—listen to the interview again and give yourself feedback. Where are you proud of how you handled follow-up questions, and where might you have missed an opportunity? What else do you notice about your technique? Come back after your first interview and use the space below to reflect on the experience.

A Review of My Interviews:

What am I most proud of from my first interview?

Can I identify a missed opportunity?

_____

_____

_____

_____

_____

_____

What kinds of questions were the most effective?

_____

_____

_____

_____

_____

_____

What is the most interesting/surprising thing I learned from this interview that I might want to further explore?

_____

_____

_____

_____

_____

_____

 ## The Final Question

The final question should always be something along the lines of "Is there anything that I didn't think to ask you that you wish I had?" or "Is there anything you want to share that we didn't get to yet?" No matter how well you prepare, there is always the chance that there is something really important in their life that you didn't know about or didn't remember to ask about. Giving them the chance to fill in anything they want to share is an important piece of the interview process and sometimes can lead to some of the best stories or insights.

 *Ethical Considerations*

Consent

Professional oral historians always have their interviewees sign a consent form. The idea is to make sure that the interviewees understand that they are participating in a research endeavor, and they know what will be done with their interviews. They agree to do the interview, and they agree that it can be donated to an archive, or used for the researcher's scholarly work, or whatever the case may be. In general, even if you may not need a legal form, making sure that everyone you interview understands what is happening and why is definitely the right thing to do.

Think about whether you might want to donate your final product to a local historical society or to share it with audiences outside your family. If you are planning on sharing your material with audiences beyond your own family, be sure to get permission from your interviewees. If you think someone in your family might be upset if they see a clip of their interview on TikTok, then you need to think through what you should and should not do with their materials.

If you decide down the road to donate a copy of your interviews to a local historical society or library, they are likely going to ask you if you have permission from the interviewees to do so. In that case, it's probably best to have a simple form, signed by your family member, that says they give you permission to do the interview and to donate the interview to a library, historical society, or archive for safekeeping and that they understand it will be made available for researchers to use. (Please note that some people, such as minors, are not legally able to give informed consent, so if you wanted to give a historical society a copy of interviews with children in your family, you'd have to get their parents' or guardians' signed consent. If you are interviewing someone who has dementia or some forms of intellectual deficits, ethically you need to think carefully about whether they understand the purpose of your interview and can give informed consent.) In most cases you could use a simple form that looks like this:

Participant's name:
Mailing address:
Phone and/or email:
I voluntarily agree to be interviewed for this family history project. I understand that the following items may be created from my interview:
• an audio and/or video recording
• an edited transcript and summary
• a photograph of me
• copies of any personal documents or additional photos that I wish to share

_____

Participant's signature/date

In addition, I understand that my interview (and other items above) may be donated to a library or archive and could be made available to the public for research and educational purposes, including in formats such as print, public programming, and the internet.

_____

Participant's signature / date

_____

Interviewer's signature / date

 *To Consider:*

Do I need to consider getting consent forms signed by my interviewees? Why or why not?

_____

_____

_____

_____

_____

_____

Tricky Situations

It's impossible to predict exactly how an interview will go; that's part of the fun. But sometimes there are situations that require some skill, tact, and sensitivity to navigate well. Always, but perhaps especially when you are interviewing family members with whom you have an ongoing relationship, you want to be sure to handle interviews in such a way that the relationship is protected and you in no way violate the person's dignity and integrity or sense of privacy.

Taking part in an oral history interview can be emotionally intense for your interviewee—after all, they are reviewing their life—but it should not feel coercive, badgering, or judgmental. Questions, and follow-up questions, should not be combative or mistrustful; you don't want the person to feel like they are in a TV police examination room. Your goal is not to create a "gotcha" moment or to lead your interviewee to "see the light" in any kind of way. (If you sense that those might be your motives, then you need to take a step back; in that case, oral history is not the right way for you to proceed.)

Even if you start an interview with all the best intentions, you can find yourself facing moments that feel difficult. The following is a list of potential situations you might find yourself in, with some tips for how to handle them.

Reluctant Narrators

In some cases, you may really want to interview somebody but at first they may not think they want to be interviewed. I once sent an email to a potential interviewee inviting her to participate in a project, and she didn't answer for weeks because she was sure it was a scam. A professional historian couldn't possibly really want to interview her, right? Sometimes people don't think they have had an interesting or important-enough life, or they fear they won't be able to remember things clearly, or they're embarrassed to be the center of attention. It's important not to pressure them—they have to willingly agree to participate. But you can explain that you are really, truly interested in their story; that it doesn't matter if there are certain dates or details they can't recall—whatever they can share with you will be enough; that they are important to you and you are eager to record their words and memories to hold and pass along to future generations. Let them take some time to think about it. Ask them what they are hesitant about, and talk it through with them. Is there anything you could do to put them more at ease?

Wandering Narrators

On the other hand, you may be blessed with a narrator who is more than happy to be interviewed and enjoys nothing more than having somebody listen to them for hours on end. In some cases, you may feel, however, that it's difficult to keep them focused on your questions—they tend to go off on tangents or launch into monologues that seem disconnected from what you are trying to get at. It's important not to interrupt them or make them feel like you are losing patience or interest. Remember that in some way or another, what they are telling you is important to them; you may not understand why or how right now, but it's very possible that you'll understand later. When they are done with a thought, you can gently guide them back to the topic at hand. "Thanks for sharing that story, Grandpa. Now, what I really want to know more about is how you got the idea to learn to fly a plane."

Untrustworthy Narrators

It may be that you have a narrator who, in one way or another, is not totally trustworthy. Perhaps they have memory issues and get mixed up about who did what and when. Remember that while you are trying to understand the past, you are also trying to understand them. You can use your background research and your other interviews to clarify points of confusion later. Depending on your relationship with them and the situation, you might be able to say, "Are you sure about that? I think maybe that was Uncle Henry, not Cousin Joe." But you can also just let it be; the most important thing is to capture their voice, their way of telling the story, their recollections and reminiscences, even if some of the details are off. For someone facing the onset of true dementia, getting the chance to record the memories and stories they do have can be a powerful experience.

In other cases, a narrator might purposely give you misleading information. Perhaps they feel shame about past behavior, or want to denigrate someone with whom they are angry. If you recognize in the moment that what they are saying is false, you can choose to gently ask some follow-up questions to probe a little bit. But rather than playing detective in the middle of the interview, it might be best to let them tell their story and then think later about how to deal with any misrepresentations. See part 3 for more on dealing with this kind of issue.

Dealing with Silences

Sometimes you will deal with silence. It might be that your interviewee takes a long pause before answering a question. Many of us are uncomfortable with silence, and you may be tempted to jump in, fill the void, or move on quickly to another question. Practice sitting still with the silence. People sometimes need time to think, to put their thoughts in order, to decide what they want to share and how they want to say it. Silence may mean that what's coming next is really important—but you have to wait for it. It can feel like it's lasting forever, but it probably is just a few seconds. Practice counting silently in your head and just waiting. As you do, show that you are still paying attention; don't rush them or look impatient. Most often, the wait will be worth it!

If you sense, after a good long wait, that the silence is their way of saying they really don't want to answer that question, then you could simply say, "If that is a topic you don't want to talk about, we can move on. Would you prefer that?"

The other kind of silence you might come across is less literal and more literary. It's the silence that comes from avoiding an issue by talking around it, by shying away from certain stories, by refocusing on different people or different times. You might ask a question about Cousin Terry, and your relative will start telling you about Terry's brother Clyde. Or you notice that your mother never really wants to talk about her experiences in high school—she skips over them quickly, going straight to when she met your father in college. Or your grandfather talks easily about his laboratory experiments, but not about how he spent his time outside of work. If you notice it during the interview, you can try to address it with a question or two. "Aunt Clara, I've noticed that people seem to avoid talking about Cousin Terry—can

you tell me why?" "Mom, I'm curious about how your friends would have described you in high school and whether that matches your own sense of yourself." "Grandpa, when you came home from the lab, how did you spend your time?" Sometimes you don't notice the absence until later when you are reviewing the interview. (That's a common type of missed opportunity!) You can decide whether to follow up with them and ask further questions—you might even do another interview if they agree— or you can simply note the issue and think about what it might reveal. Is there a pattern among the men in your family that they talk more easily about work than about family and homelife? Does your mom seem more comfortable focusing on relationships and family than on feelings of ambition or career plans?

Hearing Upsetting Stories

You might find that, when you start interviewing family members, old wounds and complicated relationships come to the forefront. You may discover that someone you have admired and loved for many years really hurt the feelings of someone else you admire and love. Or you could find out the reason nobody talks about a certain relative is because he went to jail and the family carries around a lot of shame about it. You might discover that your witty, stylish cousin is also homophobic and says things that would shock your friends. Try to remember during the interview that, for this period of time, your role is to listen, be curious, and seek to understand their experience and perspective. Your role in that interview is not to judge, to be a therapist, or to try to fix a problem. Once the interview is over, give yourself some time to think about what you heard and how you might want to handle that information in the context of your relationship and your family. You can seek out resources or specialists like therapists to help you if necessary.

Trauma

One time, I was interviewing a woman about her political career, and I asked her a simple question about her father. Suddenly, without warning, a torrential story of incest and abuse came pouring out of her, to both of our surprise. It was deeply upsetting—I wasn't sure what to do or how to handle it. I didn't think to ask if she wanted me to turn off the recorder so that she could just talk and not have it be part of the interview. Afterward, I was literally shaking; I sort of wandered around my office trying to think about what had happened. But it took me hours, days, and weeks to really process that experience.

I spent a long time looking back, trying to think how I might have handled it better. We did have a long conversation after the interview about whether she still wanted it to go in the archive, and she decided that, while she wanted it closed to researchers for quite a while, eventually she wanted the story to be made available, because she wanted other women to know that they could survive and thrive even after the worst circumstances.

It isn't always possible to know what question might trigger the memory of a traumatic experience for someone. But in other cases—for instance, if you know you are interviewing a veteran, or a survivor of domestic abuse, or the parent of a child who died young—you can assume that these will be difficult and sensitive issues to cover. You can ask them ahead of time, before the interview, if they'd be willing and able to talk about those experiences, and honor their privacy if they say no. Be sure to set up the interview in a quiet, private space. Watch and listen carefully—watch their body language, and if you sense that they are getting too emotionally triggered, you can stop—take a break, pause the recorder, get a glass of water—and if the experience is just too hard, it's okay to just say, "Why don't we set this aside." If you do face a situation like that one, you can offer to help them access resources—organizations that help people in their situation, books from the library, therapists—so that they don't have to process alone. And remember to give yourself time to process as well. Hearing traumatic stories can be extremely difficult on the interviewer—be sure to give yourself time to decompress. Seek out emotional support for yourself as well.

What tricky situation am I most worried about?

_____

_____

_____

What is one approach I might try if I do face that challenge?

_____

_____

_____

_____

_____

_____

If the interview becomes difficult, for whatever reason, to whom will I turn for support?

_____

_____

_____

_____

_____

Approaches That Can Help Navigate Some Tricky Situations

Starting with the Stuff

Starting with physical objects can be especially helpful if you have a reluctant narrator or one for whom other topics might be too unsettling to address. If your relative, for example, feels they haven't lived an "important" enough life to warrant an oral history and are reluctant to be interviewed you could focus on a set of objects. Exploring the stories attached to them, and what they reveal about your loved one's life, could be a wonderful way into this conversation. Maybe your mom has a set of beautiful ceramic pitchers that have pride of place in her kitchen. You could suggest that together you take each one down, maybe dust it, and she could tell you about it. Where did she get it? Did she buy it herself, or was it a gift? If a gift, from whom, and on what occasion? How did she feel about the gift or the purchase? What does she know about where the pitcher came from, the designs on it, or who made it? What does she remember about the phase of life she was in when she acquired it? How has she used it over the years? What or whom does it remind her of when she looks at it?

Maybe your father has a set of record albums that is his pride and joy. You could spend an afternoon going through the albums, listening to a song from each album, and asking your dad what that record means to him. What does he think of when he hears that song? In what stage of life was he when he acquired this album, and how does he feel when he listens to it? What does he remember about that point in his life? Where did he learn about that artist? Who in his life shaped his musical tastes the most? Has music been a way for him to rebel or find community or both? Why does he collect albums—when did he get started? Why does he prefer them to digital recordings? How does he think about the role of music in his life? How has that changed over time?

Perhaps your uncle is taciturn, and it's hard for you to imagine pulling him out of his shell enough to do a traditional oral history. But he has an incredible garage workshop full of tools, and the walls are lined with photographs of projects he's undertaken over the years: dollhouses for his nieces and nephews; scores of colorful, quirky birdhouses that he gave away to neighbors; and, in the rafters, a boat he built from scratch and fished out of for many years before the arthritis kicked in too badly. You could ask him to spend some time telling you about how he got into woodworking. How old was he when he first picked up a woodworking knife? Who taught him those skills—were they passed down in his family, or did he learn them in school? How did he get started, and what kept him going? What is his favorite thing about it, and has that changed over time? What does he get from woodworking that he doesn't get from his regular job? Of which project is he most proud? Did he ever think about pursuing woodworking professionally? Why or why not? How has changing technology affected the way he practices his skills?

While these approaches may not get you a linear story with a neat beginning, middle, and end, they will help you uncover the stories in the objects all around you, and they will deepen your understanding of your loved one and their past. Doing so will prevent you from feeling that dreadful sadness I experienced at my neighbor's house, when I couldn't hear what the objects wanted to tell me.

As a curator, I am always interested in the stories that objects have to tell. We can learn so much about the past from our material culture. Often museum professionals can figure out when something was made, out of what, and occasionally by whom, just by looking at it carefully and doing some research. But if we don't know how an object functioned in people's lives—what the people who owned it loved or hated about it, what they used it for, what it meant to them, why they kept it or sold it or gave it away—then we are missing most of what is important about that object's significance. Who knows, maybe someday a curator will want to collect one of your uncle's birdhouses. It might turn out that he was remarkably and unusually talented and his birdhouses are now considered wonderful specimens of "outsider art." If you have his story recorded, you will be that curator's dream come true.

Is there someone in my family who might respond best to an interview about a certain collection of objects?

How might this approach help with this particular relative?

_____

_____

_____

_____

_____

_____

Group Interviews

My grandmother had twelve aunts and uncles! I remember as a child walking into a living room and the ones who were still alive were sitting in a circle, waiting for us. I went around the room as each one said, "Hello, dear, I'm your Aunt Hannah," "Hello, dear, I'm your Aunt Bea," "Hello, dear, I'm your Aunt Julia," "Hello, dear, I'm your Aunt Pearl." Imagine what fun it would have been to interview that whole group of women together! I can just hear them laughing now. You wouldn't, perhaps, get as much detail about any one individual's life, but you'd get to hear about their shared memories, they would help fill in the gaps for one another, and you'd see their relationships on display.

Sometimes it can be helpful to do an interview with more than one person at a time. In cases where one person perhaps has a faulty memory, another can be there to support and encourage and to help when needed. You could do an interview with a married couple, or with a mother and daughter, or with a group of siblings. Of course, that might have drawbacks as well. Will the presence of one keep the other from being honest? If her husband is there, how truthfully will your grandmother talk about earlier romances?

What pairing or group of people might I want to interview together?

_____

_____

_____

_____

_____

_____

What would be the pros and cons of that approach?

_____

_____

_____

_____

_____

_____

Logistics

Now that you know how to set yourself up for success, let's get into the nuts and bolts of conducting the interview.

Setting

It's important to think about the setting for your interview. As I mentioned earlier, ideally, you'll have a room where you and your interviewee won't be interrupted and where it will be quiet. This can be a room in their home or yours; it can also be a room you reserve at the local library, or at their place of work, or maybe even in the church basement or at a friend's house. Ideally, you want somewhere there won't be dogs barking so much that it's hard to have a conversation, nor children climbing into laps and distracting you and your interviewee. It's not a good idea to do an interview in a public place—like at a coffee shop or restaurant. There will be too much background noise, and you will be interrupted too often. Once you decide on a good room, you can even put a sign on the door—"Quiet, please! Recording!" or something to that effect. One of the reasons quiet is important is so that if you get your interview transcribed, the transcriber (or, these days, often, the AI bot) can hear the voices clearly. While a little bit of noise—a teakettle whistling, a cat meowing, a wind chime—can convey a sense of the person's homelife and personality, too much will end up being a problem.

My Setting:

Where might be the best setting for my interviews?

_____

_____

_____

_____

_____

Will I need to make any special arrangements to reserve the space I need?

_____

_____

_____

_____

 Recording Devices

My brother has a remarkable memory for family stories. He loves to ask family members about the past, and the amazing thing to me is that he can retell the story, with many details intact, years later. I have long thought of him as the much better family historian in that way, collecting and passing along important pieces of our family's lore. If I, on the other hand, don't record an interview, I might very well forget much of it within a few weeks or months. If you have decided that you want to record your interviews rather than just experience them as conversations you will treasure in your own memory and pass down as family stories, then you need to decide how you are going to do so.

The simplest choice for many of us is to use the Voice Memo or Voice Recorder app that is included on most cell phones. First, if you are using a consent form, have them sign it before you start. Place the phone on a table between you and your interviewee, where it can catch both of your voices. Ideally you will plug it in, so you don't risk running out of power in the middle of the interview. (If you want to be super careful, record on two phones; that way, if there's any problem with one, you'll have a backup.) You can do a test run first, to make sure that the phone is picking up your voices clearly—press Record and say a quick hello, maybe ask your relative what they had for breakfast—and then stop recording and play it back. Once you're certain that it will work, go ahead and set it up for your interview. You simply press Record at the beginning of your interview. Do a little introduction: Say your name and the date, and introduce your interviewee—you can say what your relationship is—and maybe even where you are doing this interview. Thank your interviewee for joining you, and then get started with the questions on your interview guide.

When you are finished with the interview, thank them again for taking the time to share their story with you, and then simply press Stop. The app will give it a generic name like "Voice Memo 1," which you can change to "Uncle Henry Interview, December 15, 2026" or however you want to label it. Labels make it easier to keep track of what's what.

Then be sure to upload the file to your computer and save it to the cloud or to an external hard drive so you don't lose it if your computer crashes or you drop your cell phone into a puddle.

You can also invest in digital recorders. There are many on the market now, with prices that range greatly, but plenty are under a hundred dollars. Some now come with built-in AI transcription capability. We'll talk about transcription later. Since the technology is changing so quickly, I can only recommend that you read reviews before investing your money in one of these gadgets.

If you think you might want to do video recording, that can also be done either with your cell phone on a small tripod or with more sophisticated video cameras. You could even enlist the help of another relative who could function as your cameraperson, recording the interview as you do it. In that case, you would need to decide on whether you want the video to capture just the interviewee or both of you in the frame.

There are pros and cons to videotaping interviews. On the one hand, I think it sometimes makes people feel more self-conscious. On the other hand, it does create a wonderful record of them—their facial expressions, their surroundings, and their body language as well as their words. If you have the technology, the skills, and a room with good lighting, video might enhance your interview. But remember that you can always take a photograph of the person and share that along with an audio recording of the interview, or even with just the transcript. It depends on your goals, budget, and plans for the project. Refer back to part 1 to make sure you're still on the right track.

If you are not in the same location as your interviewee, you could, of course, do your interview over Zoom or a similar platform. You can set up a Zoom meeting, and then when you are ready to start the interview, press Record. I don't love doing interviews over Zoom—it's much harder to get a sense of the person's body language, and there is simply a less intimate feeling to the experience—but it certainly has benefits, as many of us learned during COVID. It can make all the difference if your relative lives far away and travel is difficult. And at the end of your interview, Zoom can transcribe the meeting for you using AI. But, as of this writing, Zoom transcriptions do not produce a neat document that is simple to extract and use. See the Baylor University oral history program's excellent website (https://library.web.baylor.edu/oralhistoryatadistance) for more suggestions on doing oral histories from afar, or check out their book *Oral History at a Distance*. There are also new platforms like TheirStory, which is specifically created to host oral history interviews. For a subscription fee, you can set up an account and then do Zoom-like interviews, which it will transcribe, and you can also use the platform to edit the video and create digital showcases for your work. For more information, you can visit theirstory.com.

My Recording Devices:

How do I want to record my interviews?

_____

_____

_____

_____

_____

Will I need to borrow or purchase any equipment?

_____

_____

_____

_____

_____

_____

 *Wrapping Up the Interview Process*

Field Notes

It's a great practice to write up what we call *field notes* after an interview. You'd be surprised how quickly you will forget some important details, so it's helpful to write things down immediately after the interview. You can type it on your computer, or write in your special notebook, or even record a voice memo on your phone. It doesn't take long—just record whom you interviewed, where you did the interview, the date and time, and then describe the interview itself in a few sentences or paragraphs. What were the most memorable parts? What stood out to you? Were there any parts that were confusing or problematic? Anything you wish you'd done differently?

Thank-You Note

It's a lovely idea to send a written thank-you note to each of your interviewees. After all, they've given you the gift of their time and their story. Take a moment to send them a real card with your appreciation and perhaps a word or two about your favorite moments from the interview.

 *Gathering and Sharing Stories With or Without Interviews*

Of course, there are other ways to capture family memories for future generations that are not based on interviewing people. As I mentioned earlier in this book, as a historian, I've explored several methods for documenting history, and some might be useful to you as you think about your family story.

Maybe these will enhance your journey; maybe they'll capture your imagination and lead you down another road to the same destination. The point is to collect your family's memories and record them for future generations, while strengthening your relationship in the present.

I once spent five months in Finland, from January through May 2019, as a Fulbright scholar. Besides the time I climbed down a ladder through a hole in the ice into a black lake in the dark of night to experience "winter swimming," one of the most memorable experiences was learning about *muistitieto* at the Finnish Literature Society. *Muistitieto* translates to "memory knowledge." For many generations, Finnish researchers have published questions in newspapers (for instance, "What do you remember about your experiences with nature as a child?"), and people across the country have sent in written answers, sometimes filling many pages with their memories. Those are archived at the Finnish Literature Society, where they have such records going back a hundred years.

Ever since I saw those collections, I've thought about how we might practice that here in this country. Family history seems to me a perfect place for it. You could come up with one research question every October, and ask everyone to write up their memories and send them in. For instance, "Who was your most important friend as a child, and how would you describe their role in your life?" "What chores did you have as a child, and how did those shape your attitudes toward housework?" "What do you know about how our family ended up in our hometown, and what gaps in the story do you wish we had answers for?" You could collect the submissions and read them together at Thanksgiving. You might also collect them in a three-ring binder or get them printed into a booklet at your local print shop.

Weddings offer a fantastic chance to document family stories. For instance, you could ask people to bring contributions to a time capsule project like my husband and I did. Or you could ask people to write you letters about their relationship with you and your new spouse. You could share those at the reception, or alternatively, you could vow not to read them for a decade, at which point you will open them, read them, and respond to them with a letter of your own.

You might start a family tradition where, for each birthday, the birthday celebrant contributes to a family "diary" of sorts, recounting three things they did in the last year that they are proud of, three significant family memories from that year, and three things they hope for in the year ahead. They could also reflect on what they had recorded in their last birthday entry. Over time, you'll build up a wonderful collection of family activities, shared memories, and reflections that will be treasured by those in the future.

You can also engage your broader community to document

family stories. For instance, perhaps you volunteer at a local school. You could lead a fourth-grade class or Scout troop in a project where you all work to create a community tree (rather than a traditional "family" tree). Help them learn to interview their friends and families, and come up with an interview guide that focuses not just on their own family histories but on their connections to the region or school or community. For instance, they could ask their family members about a person in the community who helped them in a time of need. What organization or institution in the community has meant the most to them over time? Not only will they learn about their own families, but they'll begin to see connections to their community as a whole.

One more thing before you go:

No matter how you decide to proceed, I hope you'll approach your project with a spirit of exploration, curiosity, and fun. So many people learned to hate history in high school when they were required to memorize a bunch of dates and names. But that's not really what history is about. History is based on asking and answering fascinating questions that help us understand change over time. You are in charge now—you get to design your own questions to help you explore the things that interest you most, with the people you love the most. Like the best road trips, this will be a memorable journey leading to amazing stories you'll treasure for the rest of your life.

Part Three

After the Interviews

In Yiddish, there is a word—*kvelling*—that means "bursting with pride and happiness." That's exactly what I was doing as I wrote this. Why? Because at the same time, my two adult daughters were coming up with their own plan for my husband's sixtieth birthday. They emailed sixty people—relatives and friends from all different chapters of his life—and asked them to send in a snippet about their dad. Each person shared a short memory that, in one way or another, captured his essence or represented a particular moment in time. Our daughters organized the submissions into chapters based on their father's stage of life (childhood, high school, college, graduate school, etc.). They designed a booklet on the website Canva, included photographs that the participants shared with them, and then had it printed and spiral-bound at a local print shop. The result is a treasure trove of memories about their father that was eye-opening for them to organize and deeply meaningful for him to read. From the childhood friend who remembered how young Benjamin excitedly stayed up late on November 11 with his brand-new digital watch to see 11:11:11 on 11/11, to the graduate school peer grateful for his unusual lack of pretension, to the former colleague who still yearned for his steady good cheer and creativity, to the new neighbor who shares his love of jazz—taken together the snippets showcase the throughlines of his character. In far too many instances, these kinds of memories and expressions of gratitude, enduring friendship, and admiration only get shared at funerals, when it is too late for the subject to hear them. I'm kvelling because my daughters were so creative, thoughtful, and effective at making sure that didn't happen here. While it wasn't a traditional work of oral history, they've absorbed the spirit of this book all on their own.

Perhaps I should not have been surprised; our girls have seen these kinds of projects since, literally, they were born. Not only are their parents historians, but their extended family shares this passion for honoring history. While my father has written several memoirs, my mother found other creative ways to pass along a sense of connection to family and the past. When our girls were born, Mom made each of them a family memory quilt. She asked each person in the family to share with her a piece of old clothing, along with a description of why they loved it or any memories associated with it. I still remember the pink-and-green flannel skirt I gave her and how I'd bought it with one of my first paychecks. The quilt included beloved family totems like my brother's old baby blanket, and even pieces of clothing from my grandparents. My mother not only sewed two beautiful quilts but assembled a little booklet to explain whom each piece of fabric represented.

Later, when the girls both demonstrated an interest in cooking, my mother compiled a family recipe book. She reached out to three generations from both sides of our family and asked for the recipes that were most associated with their family history—recipes for the foods that we grew up with, that we associate with home and love and comfort. Mom's beef stew and chicken noodle soup. My Granny's noodle kugel. My husband's Grandma's chocolate hazelnut cake. Uncle Mark's Thanksgiving butternut squash soup. Some people just submitted the recipes; others contributed little essays about the dishes and the function of food and meals in our family lives. Then Mom made copies for each family member and included blank pages where we could add more over time. These recipe books are a powerful reminder of love, memory, and history—and a practical tool that I use often!

Over the years, my mother has undertaken a variety of other family history projects, too, that help ensure memories and stories will not be lost. She transcribed a memoir that her grandfather had written by hand, so that it would be more readable to future generations, and self-published it so that we could all have copies. Most recently, she's been working on a project to compile and record the memories her mother shared with her over the years about the family farm in Ohio. My Grandmother Ruth used to spend her summers with her grandparents—immigrants from Hungary who had a farm in Lorain County, Ohio. On the weekends, they hosted Jewish families from Cleveland, providing a sort of Jewish bed-and-breakfast where families could relax and celebrate the sabbath together. My mother inherited a fabulous collection of black-and-white pictures from those days in the 1920s and '30s, when my Grandmother Ruth was just a teenager. You see her surrounded by cousins and aunts and uncles and her own grandparents; there are young and old people posing in and on great old cars, riding a tractor and a horse, boating on a river, and feeding chickens and geese. My mother is typing up all the stories she remembers her mom telling her about the farm and compiling them alongside the photographs so that we can all have this important piece of family history. I'm eagerly awaiting our copy of the final project!

My mother also collects blue-and-white commemorative plates to document each place one of us has lived. She has plates from Ohio, Minnesota, Connecticut, Wisconsin, New York, Massachusetts—and we have fun sharing memories of each place around the dinner table whenever they appear. The plates prompt memories from places we may have left long ago but that were home at some point.

My mom's efforts are, each in their own way, examples of how you can collect, record, and share family history. She used oral history methods, alongside other creative techniques; she reached out to family, asked questions, and shared the results with us. In the process, she both documented family history for the future and deepened bonds in the present. My mother infuses history into so many moments of family togetherness that it doesn't even seem remarkable to us. The impact, as my daughters' birthday project for my husband recently reminded me, is powerful. Your projects can play a similar role in your family.

 *Putting It All Together*

Let's imagine you've done some background research—perhaps you went to the library, talked to a librarian, read some books and articles, and took good notes, either on a computer or in the special notebook you chose just for this purpose. You decided who in your family you wanted to interview, and you created interview guides. You made the time to sit down with your family members, and you listened closely as they told you their stories and memories. Maybe you even asked some great follow-up questions, and the interviews went better than you could have hoped. You recorded them on your phone, and now you have these wonderful MP3 files with your loved ones' voices. So, now what?

What kind of presentation will do justice to all your good work? For many people, there is something compelling about the idea of writing up family history in the form of a book.

But for others, that prospect feels overwhelming. As I hope my family's examples suggest, there are many creative ways to share your history, and I hope you will have as much fun as we all have coming up with new ways to incorporate the past into your family traditions.

In this part of the book, I suggest some different ways to approach sharing your family history after you have gathered it. I offer some advice for organizing your interviews and, if you want, writing up your research in book format. If a long writing project is not your thing, I also provide alternative ideas for family history projects that I hope will inspire you. You can follow the steps I lay out below, or you can use these suggestions as a starting point and come up with your own creative approach to sharing what you've learned.

Getting Organized

Create and Organize Your Files

First, upload those interview files onto a computer. On your computer, create folders that will help you stay organized. For instance, you might have a folder with "Family History Project," and then subfolders for "Notes on Background Readings," "Interview Guides," and "Interview Audio Files." Upload the MP3 files into that last folder. Name each file with the name of the person interviewed and the date of the interview. (If you are only doing one interview, this may be overkill. If you are doing many interviews, you could alternatively organize your files by person, so you would have a folder for Grandma Jean, Grandpa George, and Uncle Charlie, and then you would upload all the relevant materials into those folders.)

How I'll Stay Organized:

How might I organize my research files? How do I want to name my folders?

_____

_____

_____

_____

_____

_____

Transcribe Your Interviews

The next step I highly suggest is that you get those audio files transcribed. Transcriptions will make it much easier to work with your interviews, and they are a richly important historical document in and of themselves. While audio interviews are fabulous and powerful, they do take a long time to listen to, so it is helpful to have a written version that someone can read—and that you can search for terms in—or copy and paste from in your history projects.

There are a few ways to go about transcribing interviews. You can do it yourself—that requires that you listen to the interview and type up what you hear as you go. It's harder than it sounds and takes a long time, but you will become intimately familiar with the interviews, and it's a wonderful learning experience. It gives you a chance to review your own method as an interviewer. Were your questions clear and open-ended? Did you ask good follow-up questions? Did you manage to keep the focus on them, or did you start to talk too much at some point? It will also give you a chance to listen closely again to what your interviewees were saying, and maybe you'll hear things in a new way this time. You might notice a recurring theme—maybe it strikes you that your cousin often seems to refer to a childhood accident, and you realize that perhaps that event played a much bigger role in her life than you had understood. It is, however, a time-consuming job, and if you have the budget, you can pay somebody else to do it for you—there are still individuals out there who make a living by transcribing. These professionals are excellent and can transcribe interviews much more quickly and accurately than most of us can, but the price can be prohibitive if you have a lot of interviews to transcribe. AI is becoming better and better at transcribing—it is the fastest and cheapest way to go, but it is not as reliable as human transcribers yet. It's a remarkable tool, but it still has a tendency to make pretty significant mistakes, like mixing up the speakers and attributing the quotes to the wrong person, not understanding dialect or accents, or even making up whole new words or passages. There are some places online where you can have AI do some transcribing for free, like Descript. There are also companies like Rev that will use AI to transcribe an interview quickly, and then you can pay extra to have it reviewed by human editors. You could also have an AI transcript created relatively cheaply and then review and edit the interview transcript yourself. In any case, I do recommend reading the transcript carefully to look for mistakes; you can catch some just by reading, but others may require that you listen to the audio and read the transcript at the same time. You may even need to ask your interviewee for help if you can't understand a word they said or aren't sure how to spell a long-lost aunt's name.

One thing to consider is that there are different types of transcripts. One is "verbatim," which means that it is the literal transcription of everything each person said—including all the *um*s, the coughs, the times somebody circled back and restarted their sentence. The other type of transcript is *not* verbatim but smooths out those jagged parts and makes it easier to read. This kind of "cleaned-up" transcript should remain as true to the speaker's voice as possible but can help make it easier to read so that their ideas and stories come across clearly. "Um, well, I used to—well, I used to work at the store on Tuesdays after school until—[*cough*] Excuse me, until I graduated" would become "I used to work at the store on Tuesdays after school until I graduated." With professional transcribers or online services, you can request verbatim or non-verbatim transcripts.

Another option to consider is an index to the interview. Rather than a full transcription, an index offers brief summaries of the focus of the conversation at each point in time, and occasionally inserts memorable quotes from each section. So, for instance, it might look something like this:

Minutes 1–10: Childhood in Tennessee

Minutes 10–12: Trip to Dollywood

Minutes 13–20: Leaving home for college

00:14:35 "I thought my heart might break when I saw Mama crying as we pulled out of the driveway."

Deciding How I'll Transcribe My Interviews:

What is my budget for this project?

_____

_____

_____

_____

_____

What is my time frame for this project?

_____

_____

_____

_____

_____

What is my bandwidth for this project?

_____

_____

_____

_____

_____

_____

Do I want verbatim or non-verbatim transcripts?

_____

_____

_____

_____

_____

_____

Do I want to transcribe my own interviews? If not, what technology do I have access to, and how can it help me further this project?

_____

_____

_____

_____

_____

_____

_____

Once you have your interviews transcribed and edited, you should upload those into a folder that you create inside your "Family History Project" folder, either in the folder for the correct person or in a general folder called something like "Interview Transcripts."

Sharing What You've Learned

How do you want to share your research with your family or other audiences? As we have discussed, there are a variety of options, and choosing the right one will depend on many factors, including your:

* Motivation
* Audience
* Scope
* Resources
* Format

Hopefully, as we discussed in part 1, you gave this some thought before you began your interviews so that you can avoid problems like wishing you could make a documentary film but only having audio instead of video. But this is a good moment to take stock again and think about what you learned during your research, what kinds of materials you've gathered, and what excites you most about how to proceed. Below are some ideas to consider.

A Collection of Interview Transcripts

One relatively simple project is to collect the transcripts of your interviews together into a booklet. You could gather together all the edited transcripts and then provide as much, or little, contextual information as you want.

You might decide to write an introduction that could help explain the project for future readers: Why did you decide to do these interviews? Whom did you interview and when? What are some overall takeaways from the interviews? What do you hope your readers will learn from reading them? You might point out some interesting themes that emerge from across the interviews—perhaps you want your readers to notice how profoundly religion has shaped your family's experience, or you want to highlight that many different interviewees all talked about the importance of education, or how deeply so many members of your family feel connected to the land.

You could pull your introduction and the interviews together into a document and then have it printed. You could simply put it in a three-ring binder or other inexpensive report cover, or you could have it professionally bound at a local copy shop. If you want to do something more involved, and perhaps add photographs or other illustrations, you could work with online services to design and print and bind your book. My daughter used Canva.com to design and print the book for her dad's birthday; there are others available with a quick Google search.

If you have done a significant amount of historical background research, you may want to share the fruits of your labor with your readers. You could write up what you learned as part of your introduction—providing background and context for the interviews—and provide footnotes and a bibliography so that your audiences can follow your lead if they want to learn more. Perhaps you've done background reading on the history of your town or on one of the themes or turning points mentioned in part 1, and you think it would help your readers to know some of what you learned. For instance, perhaps you read about the impact of the women's rights movement in the 1960s and '70s, and what you read helped you see your grandmother's, mother's, and aunt's stories in a new light. You could include some of that information in the introduction and explain why you found it relevant and interesting in light of your own family's experiences. As we discussed in part 1, be sure to credit the secondary or primary sources to which you referred.

A Book About Your Family History

Do you yearn to be an author? Perhaps you'd prefer to write up the results of your research and interviews in the form of a family history or memoir. This is a more involved endeavor, but one that is ideal for you if you have more time, are deeply invested in the process, and will enjoy the challenge of organizing your ideas and writing. There isn't one right or wrong way to write your family's history, and your choices will be shaped by what you have learned as you did your research and interviews. Below, I give you some suggestions for different approaches you can take; you will make your choice based on what appeals to you and which one you think will make the best use of the material you have.

If you are writing up your research rather than sharing the transcripts with your family, the approach to your interviews is different. You will use quotes or excerpts from your interviews, placed into the context of sections or chapters you write; you'll likely draw from several interviews for each chap ter. Each section or chapter will have a focus, and your job will be to draw some conclusions from your research and then use quotes from what you've read and from your interviews as evidence.

The first step in this case is to review all your background research and your interviews and see what emerges. What stands out to you as the most interesting thread? Are you struck most by the narrative of your family's change over time? Or are you most fascinated by themes that seem to wind their way through multiple generations? Are there major turning points in your family's trajectory, or are you more interested in showcasing individual characters and the roles they've played in your family history? Answering these questions can help you decide how to organize your book.

Brainstorming a Book About
My Family History:

What do I find most interesting about my interviews?

_____

_____

_____

_____

_____

What themes do I see running throughout them?

_____

_____

_____

_____

_____

What are major turning points in my family's trajectory?

_____

_____

_____

_____

_____

_____

Who are characters that might play a central role in our family's story?

_____

_____

_____

_____

_____

_____

How would I describe change over time in my family's history?

_____

_____

_____

_____

_____

_____

Once you have reviewed your research and your interviews, you can think through how to structure your book's approach. Do you want chapters based on chronology, themes, or characters? For example, if you chose chronological chapters, in each one, you would write about how your family experienced that particular time period (such as the 1960s and '70s), and you could pull quotes from multiple different interviewees who discuss their memories of those particular decades. The same would work if you decided to organize your book around particular turning points or phases in your family's own history (such as before and after they moved from South Carolina to Chicago).

If, after reviewing your interviews, you are struck by themes that emerge, you could choose to write chapters that focus on them—perhaps topics like education, health and sickness, marriage and family, religion—and pull from different interviews to show how members of your family have experienced and talked about those issues.

Another possibility is to organize the book based on individuals in your family. So, for instance, a chapter might be focused around your grandmother. Perhaps you interviewed her, and you can pull together background research you did on her life, highlights from your interview, and quotes from other interviews you did in which people talk about events or memories that involved her.

Your plan may shift as you develop your ideas. I wrote a book based on interviews with women who were active in the feminist movement around 2012–2016.* Originally, I thought I'd organize the book into chapters based on their professions; whether they worked in nonprofits, academia, the corporate world, or philanthropy. But over time, I decided that the most interesting way to see connections among them and differences between them was to group the interviews by their ages— activists who were in their twenties, thirties, or forties at the time of our interview. You can play around with different ideas to see what starts to make most sense to you and will allow you to convey what you believe to be your most important findings.

---

* Rachel F. Seidman, *Speaking of Feminism: Today's Activists on the Past, Present and Future of the U.S. Women's Movement* (University of North Carolina Press, 2019).

Brainstorming a Book About My Family History, Continued:

How might I organize my chapters? By decade, character, theme?

_____

_____

_____

_____

_____

Where would my book begin and end?

_____

_____

_____

_____

_____

Where might I find photographs or other images to illustrate my book?

_____

_____

_____

_____

_____

Consider Looking Beyond the Confines
of Your Family

I'd like to encourage you to connect your family's story to the larger history of the country. Use your background research and reading to help place your family's experiences into historical context. If your family's history was deeply shaped by the loss of the family farm in the 1930s, for instance, it's important to point out that it was the Depression, and many farms were lost. This was not a personal failing but a societal and political one. You could look back at local newspapers from the time, or read histories of that period, to help show how your family's experience was shaped by the economics and politics of the time. If your great-grandfather, a World War II veteran, was the first person in his family to go to college, you can celebrate him and connect his achievement to the GI Bill that supported education for veterans. While some turning points might be unique to your family, in many cases, our personal histories are deeply shaped by what was happening around us, and we make decisions within a larger framework that is important to understand. You can help members of your family grasp that broader context by sharing the results of your historical research in this format.

How I Could Incorporate Historical Context:

Which historical events might I need to explain that have informed my family's story?

_____

_____

_____

_____

What historical context will I want to be sure to include as I write up my family research?

_____

_____

_____

_____

_____

How might putting our story into the larger narrative of our local, regional, or national history help us understand our own family's experience?

_____

_____

_____

_____

Choosing What to Share

Just as you need to be prepared to deal with some difficult moments during interviews, you may also want to think through some potentially tricky aspects of writing up your family history.

How will you handle competing memories of the same event or person? People's memories are fallible, and how they recall events in the distant or even more recent past can be shaped by a variety of factors. What happens if your brother insists that your childhood home was painted green, but you remember it as blue? In some cases, you might be able to use historical evidence to establish some facts—for instance, an old photograph could help you determine the color. (Maybe it was bluish green!)

In other cases, conflicting memories are not as simple to resolve. What will you do if Uncle Joe says that his parents' fiftieth wedding anniversary was wonderful, but his brother remembers it as miserable—that their parents bickered at the reception, and everyone left early? What if one person says that Great-Aunt Harriet was horribly grouchy, but another person remembers her as witty and droll? You'll want to think through your options. Sometimes you can simply point out that we all experience people and events differently, and that families are full of individuals who see the world from slightly different angles. You could also make the differing memories a focal point of your story if you think that is particularly interesting or relevant.

In some cases, though, you might decide there is more to lose from focusing on dissension than there is to gain from the retelling of a particular story. Perhaps, even though you have uncovered this intriguing conflict in how people remember that wedding anniversary, you might keep that to yourself and just choose not to highlight that information in your final product. Those kinds of decisions—about how much painful family history to share versus when to let sleeping dogs lie— are likely to come up. Every family has its share of pain and conflict alongside the love and loyalty. Depending on your family, your situation, and your goals, you will need to decide on how much of the former to surface.

How I'll Choose What to Put In, and What to Leave Out:

What are some difficult decisions I might need to make in writing about my family's history?

_____

_____

_____

_____

How might I address some of these issues?

_____

_____

_____

_____

_____

_____

What worries me the most?

_____

_____

_____

_____

_____

What could I do to mitigate those fears?

_____

_____

_____

_____

_____

_____

How can I balance honesty and valuing family harmony?

_____

_____

_____

_____

_____

_____

Editing

Every writer needs a good editor. Some people are nervous about sharing their writing with another person, perhaps scarred by too many red pen marks on school papers in their youth. I remember in college thinking that I *should* be able to write a chapter of my senior thesis and get it back from my professor with a simple "Good job!" But thankfully, I've learned that isn't really how writing works. Every author you've ever read has had an editor—often several—and they play an important role. They help you see what you're too close to the material to catch; they give you an outsider's perspective, making it easier to understand what makes sense to a reader and what might be confusing; they can give you honest feedback on what else you might need to say to get your point across clearly. My college professor gave me wonderful, thoughtful, challenging advice that helped me learn to think and write like a historian. So even though I might have been discouraged to see so many comments in the margins, the result was a paper that in fundamental ways launched me into the rest of my career, and to her, I am eternally grateful.

So don't avoid enlisting an editor. It can be someone in the family—maybe you want your sister's advice on how to handle some of the more complicated family dynamics. Or you could have a friend—ideally somebody who writes well or who reads a lot—read your draft and ask them to tell you where your writing is unclear, or if you've repeated content, or whether they think you need to add more explanation of the broader context.

You can also hire editors. A freelance editor will charge you a fee, but you'll be getting a professional's advice. If you are struggling with how to organize your material, how to structure your chapters, or how to incorporate your interviews and background research, you could hire a developmental editor—they focus on the content and the big picture. They can read what you've done and give you advice on how to proceed and will let you know if they think there is a better way to go about it. If you feel generally happy with your manuscript but want to make sure your writing and organization are clear and there are no problems with style, grammar, or spelling, then you want a copy editor. And if all you really want is somebody to scour the book for any grammatical or spelling mistakes at the very end, what you need is a proofreader. If you are working with a freelance editor, you want to make clear which kind of editing you are looking for. They'll most likely charge you based on the word count of your manuscript and the kind of feedback you want. You can find freelance editors in a variety of ways, but one place to start is the Editorial Freelancers Association, where you can post a description of your project and interested freelancers can contact you.

These days, it is also possible to feed your chapters into AI and ask it to check for clarity, spelling, grammar, and the like. While it can be a helpful tool, just like with transcription, you should not rely on AI completely for editing. You'll still want to have real people read your work and give you honest feedback and check for mistakes (including mistakes that your chatbot made).

After you receive feedback from your editor(s), your task is to revise your manuscript. You do not have to do everything they tell you—it is, after all, your book. But try to consider their responses as helpful suggestions rather than as criticism and incorporate the ones that make sense to you.

Self-Publishing

Once you have a manuscript that you are happy with, you'll want to share it with others. If you want something more formal than a document you print out at home, you can look online for print-on-demand services that will help you design and self-publish your book. In that case, you'll you'll end up with what looks like a traditional book, with a cover. You can choose whether to print just one copy or many to give to friends and family. You can also set it up so that family members can order their own copies in the future. As we discussed in part 1, there might be local organizations— like your local historical society, congregation, or school library—that would like to have a copy of your book as well. You might want to ask them, however, before you spend

money printing your book, in case they don't accept dona-
tions like that.

Alternatives to a Book

What if you want to do something more than just print out
the interview transcripts, but you don't feel up to writing a
book, or don't think that is the best vehicle to help you reach
your goals? Don't worry—there are lots of other options! Did
you know that middle and high school students all across
the country participate in National History Day competitions? They choose how to present their research from a list
of options, including documentaries, exhibits, websites, and
performances. Those are all great ideas! And I've got more suggestions for you below, as well.

Just like students at National History Day, you can choose
whether to work alone or with a group. As I mentioned earlier in the book, this is a great time to ask your family for
help. Perhaps you'd like to enlist relatives to join your project. Maybe your niece has excellent computer skills; maybe
your nephew loves creative writing; maybe your sister-in-
law is a terrific graphic designer. Bringing family together to
work on a family history project has its own inherent benefits of sharing stories, time, and hopefully some good laughs
together.

Documentary

If you have video editing skills—or want to learn them—you could consider making a documentary film about your family history. If you videotaped your interviews, you can edit clips of them together, with historical photographs and documents, and perhaps voice-over narration. There are lots of guides online for getting started, including advice about the kinds of software you'll need, and there are also classes and workshops you can take to learn more. National History Day offers some tips and resources online; they might be a useful place to begin.

Website

How about creating a family history website? There are some sites like Ancestry that seek to help genealogists share their research with audiences. You could use one of those, or you could use a more general website-creation tool kit and build what you need from there. Again, you could include photographs, copies of historical documents, and clips from your interviews, whether they are audio or video.

Exhibit

Maybe you have an upcoming family reunion, and you want to share your findings with your relatives in a fun, interactive way at the event itself. You could take your cue from National History Day students, who create exhibits on trifold boards, similar to what you may have seen at a science fair. While these cardboard-based exhibitions are not likely to last forever, if your goal is to share your family history at a particular event, then an exhibit could be a great way to go. You could include photographs, copies of historical documents, and quotes from your inter-views. Just like with a book, you need to choose a clear way to organize your information. Remember that for an exhibition, you will have room for far fewer words—so you'll need to be judicious. You could, though, include audio clips from your interviews on an iPad or similar device that your audience could listen to on headphones while they look at the exhibition.

Performance

You could be inspired by my Aunt Helen's wedding gift of a musical based on interviews about my husband and me and write a play about your own family's history—with or without catchy songs! You don't have to come up with a whole narrative plot—although that would be great. It's actually a powerful method to simply pull quotes from different interviews and put them in "conversation" with one another. For instance, perhaps in the interviews you did, you have multiple family members remembering how they spent their childhood summers, across different generations. You could have performers share those memories—perhaps they all take place at the same summer camp, but in different decades; or perhaps they all revolve around "the lake" or showcase the summer jobs people had, from picking cucumbers in the hot sun to scooping ice cream to lifeguarding at the local pool. You can enlist family members to read their own quotes, or have other family members read them and let the interviewees relax in the audience. No matter how you organize your performance, it's bound to be a joyous family occasion when you gather and share it.

Family History Podcast

Another project could be editing a family history podcast. Again, you have choices to make about how to proceed. Do you want to share long excerpts from single interviews? You could have different "episodes" about each person you interviewed. You might do a brief introduction as the "host" and then splice together the best parts of the interview. Or, you could have episodes about different moments in time— say one on the 1960s, one on the 1980s, and one on the 2000s—and pull quotes from several people's interviews about memorable events in those eras. Or you could center your episodes on different themes. Imagine one episode about love stories from across the generations, another about memories of school, one about work, and one about leisure time activities. Audio editing is a skill and takes some time to learn, but with all the great online tools out there, such as Audacity or Descript, you can do it. You can create your podcast and upload it on Spotify for Creators, or on Soundcloud, and then either share it just with your family members or more broadly.

Recipe Books and a Potluck Meal

Perhaps, like my mom, you are interested in collecting your family's food history. Either as a stand-alone project or as part of broader oral history interviews, you could ask your family questions about the role of food in their lives and about specific dishes. Where did their family do their grocery shopping? Did they grow or produce any of their own food? What do they remember about the kitchen in the home where they grew up? What foods did their grandparents and parents often make? What were special occasion dishes? How was your family's ethnic, racial, religious, or regional heritage passed down through food? What do they consider comfort food and why? What family recipes do they continue to cook at home? You could collect the recipes into a booklet and add quotes from the interviews to go alongside them. You might even host a potluck and ask everyone to bring one of the dishes they talked about, and then share the booklet and the stories over a family meal. Give family members a copy of the recipe book as a gift to take home with them!

Quilts and Storytelling

If you are skilled at crafts, you might think about creating a quilt. There is a long tradition of quilts being a way for people to capture and share family history through the reuse of fabrics and artistry. The quilts my mom made for my daughters when they were born, using fabric from clothing items contributed by family members, is a great example. Perhaps you could build on that model and incorporate quotes from family interviews, whether printed on fabric or hand embroidered. Quilting can be either a solo or a collaborative endeavor, and a family-history-sharing quilting bee could be a fabulous new tradition for you to try.

 *You're on Your Way!*

Do you remember those *Choose Your Own Adventure* books, where at various points in the story you got to make a decision, like whether to go into the dark cave or stay outside and walk toward the beach? Think of this process like that—there is no one right way to tell your family's story. But there are choices you can make that will get you to where *you* want to go.

Maybe you know exactly where you want to go now that

you've reached this part of the book. Or perhaps you're still weighing the options I've listed (I know there are quite a few!). If you're choosing between a few formats, maybe the imaginary example below of someone thinking through their project will help you decide what might work best for you:

Why did I undertake this project, and what are my goals at this stage?

I wanted to preserve the voices and the memories of the oldest generation in my family, the three living Johnson siblings, and to learn more from them about their experiences growing up, their parents, and their older brother, who died in the Korean War. I did research on the Korean War, and I interviewed my mother and her two sisters. Now I want to share what I've learned with my family and to use this project as a way to deepen our family's sense of connection to one another and our own past.

What will interest my audience?

The adults in my family will love all of it, but the kids might be most interested in the stories about feeding the chickens and gathering the eggs before going to school, the neighborhood jump rope competitions, Aunt Jeannie's purple birthday cake, and the puppy she got when she turned eight. I want them to know about Uncle Robert, who died so young, but don't want to upset them too much.

What do I have time for?

I have plenty of time because I'm retired.

What do I have money for?

I have a small budget but want to keep this frugal. I could get my interviews transcribed by AI, but then I would edit them myself. I could pay a small fee to get something printed.

What do I have talent for and interest in?

I love history, and I'm a pretty decent writer. I have some computer skills and would like to learn about using online design sites. I am not particularly artistic, but I have a daughter who draws really well who might contribute some illustrations.

If I were talking to this person, I might give them the following advice for a multipart project:

1. I suggest you produce a printed booklet of your interview transcriptions, with an introduction that you write providing context drawn from some of your research, such as what you learned about the Korean War, what American troops faced there, and how many soldiers died. Include photographs of the three living siblings and of their long-lost brother.

2. Devise a playlist of your three interviews and share with everyone in your family on Spotify or Soundcloud so they can listen to them when and where they want.

3. Create a children's booklet that pulls from the longer interviews the specific stories you think your younger family members would find most interesting. If you are feeling creative, you could even retell the stories in the third person and have them illustrated by your daughter—voilà, your own children's book!

4. Host a family dinner, perhaps during a holiday, where you distribute the booklets. After dinner you can listen together to some of the most compelling parts of the interviews and talk about what you heard. Encourage everyone to ask more questions. Sit back and enjoy your family's exploration of their own history and how it connects to the larger history of this country and the world.

As you can see, there are lots of different ways to share your family story. You really can't choose a wrong path; they all end up somewhere great. Select a project design that engages you, that will make use of your talents (and those of your family members), meet your goals, and entertain your audience. Enlist help and consider the process as important as the outcome. Recording and sharing your family history with your loved ones is a generous gesture and one that will have ongoing ripple effects throughout the generations. It's going to be fun; enjoy the ride!

Conclusion

Writing this book helped me see my own family in a new way. Before I started, I hadn't quite realized how strongly the thread of family history-keeping weaves through our way of being in the world together. Perhaps in part because of the silences and lost histories of the generations before us who came over from eastern Europe, we seem, each in our own way, to embrace this practice. I've been incredibly lucky to grow up surrounded by people who value history and who express love in part by collecting and sharing stories about the past.

You may or may not come from a family like mine. But I like to imagine what you might do now that you've read this book. I see some of you heading to your public library, notebook in hand. The friendly reference librarian looks up from her desk and smiles when you start to ask great questions about where you can find more information about your town's local history.

I see others of you pulling out your phones, finding the Voice Memo app on them, and testing it out. Maybe you say a few words into it, or capture the sound of your baby granddaughter babbling as she plays with the plastic cups you gave her. You start to think about how easy it would be, really, to start recording some of your family members' memories. Some of you are looking around your house, thinking about the objects in it, maybe with a new set of questions in mind. Every day, you see that framed print on the wall that came from your mom's trip to Japan, but you realize you don't know what her favorite memories are from that vacation, and you're starting to make a plan. I see stacks of new family heirlooms—bound copies of interview transcripts wrapped and ready to give away as gifts. I hear some of you talking about starting a new tradition like adding an episode to a family history podcast every Thanksgiving, or writing a new song each year about an event in your family's past to be performed together on New Year's Eve.

In a world where we can easily feel disconnected from one another, where we hear more sound bites than stories, where we post quick, selectively shiny updates about ourselves online, it is deeply rewarding to slow down, dig deeper, and draw closer to one another by listening more carefully and sharing memories. I hope this book helps you feel confident in your ability to do so. I hope you have fun, strengthen your family ties, and find creative ways to ensure that your family's story lives on.

I'm cheering you on—I believe wholeheartedly that you can do this, that it will be a meaningful experience for you, and that your whole family will benefit. As a historian, I'm grateful to you for undertaking the work; we need family history-keepers! Your work lays an incredibly important foundation in both documenting the past and helping your family see why it matters. You already have a sense of what I'm sure you will come to appreciate even more deeply through this process—that an understanding of the past and how our own personal stories fit into a longer and wider context is a building block for being a good family member, community member, and citizen. When I imagine all of you out there recording and sharing your families' histories, in my mind's eye, I see a quilt; each of you carefully and creatively crafting a square about your own family's story. Stitch them all together and we get *our* story.

Acknowledgments

To my beloved parents, Irv and Linda Seidman, you are the foundation on which this book, and my life, rests. You inspired so much of how I approached this work; I hope you see yourselves reflected and honored in this new chapter of our family history-keeping.

To my long-distance gardening buddy and longtime friend Jill Lepore, thank you for insisting I take on this project and for your generous, cheerful encouragement along the way; this book would not have happened without you. To my editor at Simon & Schuster, Emily Graff, thank you for having faith in me from our very back-of-the-napkin beginning, and for making it so fun to bring this book to completion. To editorial assistant Katie McClimon, thank you for being consistently patient, optimistic, and supportive, and for keeping us on track. To Miki Lowe, thank you for bringing my ideas to life with your gorgeous cover and illustrations. To the entire team at Simon Element, thank you for putting everything together and thank you to Carah Gedeon, Ali Kochik, and Jessica Preeg for helping spread the word out in the world. To my agent, Gillian MacKenzie, thank you for your infectious enthusiasm for this project and for your guidance helping me craft the best possible approach from the very start.

To my Oberlin College senior thesis advisor, Carol Lasser, and her husband and fellow historian Gary Kornblith, my longtime cheerleaders, and to my mentors and colleagues in oral history, Jacquelyn Dowd Hall, Bob Korstad, Della Pollock, Malinda Maynor Lowery, Renée Alexander Craft, Kathy Williams, Jaycie Vos, Sara Wood, Samir Meghelli, Jennifer Morris, Miriam Doutriaux, Kelly Elaine Navies, Ben Gillespie, and Anne Heimo, thank you for all the knowledge you've so generously shared with me over the years and for the joy of our shared belief in the power of people's stories. Thank you as well to Robert Maloy who generously shared his research on AI and oral history, and to my niece Susannah Broun, who shared her expertise on podcasting.

And, of course, to my husband, Benjamin Filene, my heartfelt thanks for joyfully, creatively, and generously sharing a love of history and family with me for close to forty years, and to our daughters, Eliza and Hazel, for being your own remarkable selves and carrying on our traditions in your own ways. Eliza and our dear son-in-law Khalid Williams have my special gratitude for bringing Ida C. Williams into the world and giving our family a particularly darling reason to document the past and celebrate the future.

Additional Reading

Here I've suggested a few books that provide helpful overviews of American history that are written for popular (not academic) audiences. I also offer recommendations for other books, websites, and resources that I mention in the text or that will help you dive deeper into some of the topics we discussed. These are just a few suggestions; visit your public library for more!

United States History

Jill Lepore, *These Truths: A History of the United States* (W. W. Norton, 2018).

Depression and World War II

David M. Kennedy, *Freedom from Fear: The American People in Depression and War, 1929–1945* (Oxford University Press, 2001).

Emily Yellin, *Our Mothers' War: American Women at Home and at the Front During World War II* (Free Press, 2004).

1950s, '60s, and '70s

James T. Patterson, *Grand Expectations: The United States, 1945–1974* (Oxford University Press, 1997).

Isabel Wilkerson, *The Warmth of Other Suns: The Epic Story of America's Great Migration* (Vintage, 2011).

Gail Collins, *When Everything Changed: The Amazing Journey of American Women from 1960 to the Present* (Little, Brown, 2009).

1970s–2000s

James T. Patterson, *Restless Giant: The United States from Watergate to Bush v. Gore* (Oxford University Press, 2007).

Oral History Methodology and Readings on Related Topics

Donna M. DeBlasio et al., *Catching Stories: A Practical Guide to Oral History* (Swallow Press, 2009).

Valerie Yow, *Recording Oral History: A Guide for the Humanities and Social Sciences* (Rowman & Littlefield, 2014).

Donald A. Ritchie, *Doing Oral History* (Oxford University Press, 2014).

For listening to oral histories: Oral History Online, https://search.alexanderstreet.com/orhi.

More sample questions: List of Life History Questions from the Southern Oral History Program at the University of North Carolina, https://sohp.org/wp-content/uploads/2022/12/Life-History-Questions.pdf.

Handling trauma in oral history from the National Park Service: "Case Study: Interviewing about Difficult Topics," https://www.nps.gov/articles/000/oral-history-resources-interviewing-difficult-topics.htm.

How to do oral histories when you are far away from your interviewees, including a great list of useful software, apps, and tools: Steven Sielaff, Stephen M. Sloan, Adrienne A. Cain Darough, and Michelle Holland, *Oral History at a Distance* (Routledge, 2024).

Website: https://library.web.baylor.edu/oralhistoryatadistance.

The Oral History Association has resources and guides you can access online: https://oralhistory.org/.

Quilting and Family History

Regina Abernathy, *The Quilting Storyteller: Preserving African American Culture and History through Quilting Stories* (independently published, 2023), available on Amazon.

Deb Rowden, *Quilter's Stories: Collecting History in the Heart of America* (C&T Publishing, 2005).

Elise Schebler Roberts, *The Quilt: A History and Celebration of an American Art Form* (Voyageur Press, 2007).

You can listen to some excerpts of oral histories and read a blog post about quilting from the Library of Congress here: https://blogs.loc.gov/families/2024/01/quilts-and-quilting -piecing-together-family-history/

Reading on Stories about Material Culture

Kimber Thomas, "Makeshifting: Black Women and Resilient Creativity in the Rural South," *Southern Cultures*, Spring 2020, https://www.southerncultures.org/article /makeshifting/.

Research, Interviewing, and Transcription Tools

Rev (https://www.rev.com/).

Descript (https://www.descript.com/).

TheirStory (https://www.theirstory.io/)

TurboScribe (https://turboscribe.ai/)

Tropy (https://www.tropy.org).

Archival and Genealogy Research Guides

Laura Schmidt, "Using Archives: A Guide to Effective Research," Society of American Archivists, updated March 26, 2012, https://www2.archivists.org/usingarchives.

"Free Genealogy Websites," National Genealogical Society, https://www.ngsgenealogy.org/free-resources/websites/.

"Free Resources," National Genealogical Society, https://www .ngsgenealogy.org/free-resources/.

"Getting Started," National Genealogical Society, https://www.ngsgenealogy.org/getting-started/.

Ancestry (https://www.ancestry.com/).

Selected List of Online Primary Source Collections

Gilder Lehrman Institute American History (https://www.gilderlehrman.org/collection/research).

Smithsonian Online Virtual Archives (https://sova.si.edu/).

National Archives (https://www.archives.gov/research).

Library of Congress (https://www.loc.gov/discover/).

New York Public Library (https://archives.nypl.org/).

How to Organize Research and Citations

Zotero (https://www.zotero.org/).

Chicago Manual of Style (https://www.chicagomanualofstyle.org/tools_citationguide.html).

Other Works I Mention in This Book

Margareta Magnusson, *The Gentle Art of Swedish Death Cleaning: How to Free Yourself and Your Family from a Lifetime of Clutter* (Scribner, 2018).

Tennessee Williams, *The Glass Menagerie* (New Directions, 1999).

Irv Seidman, *Interviewing as Qualitative Research: A Guide for Researchers in Education and the Social Sciences*, 5th ed. (Teachers College Press, 2019).

Rachel Seidman, *Speaking of Feminism: Today's Activists on the Past, Present and Future of the U.S. Women's Movement* (University of North Carolina Press, 2019).

Index

About the Author

Rachel F. Seidman, PhD, is an award-winning curator and a professional oral historian. She is a curator at the Smithsonian American Women's History Museum. Seidman directed the Southern Oral History Program at the University of North Carolina Chapel Hill and taught history there, at Duke University, and at Carleton College. In 2019, Seidman was a Fulbright Scholar at the University of Turku, Finland. She holds a PhD in history from Yale University, and a BA from Oberlin College. She is the author of *Our Story* and *Speaking of Feminism.*